BY THE AUTHOR

BOOKS

How to Make Money in Real Estate with Government Loans and Programs

Hidden Fortunes

How to Manage Real Estate Successfully—in Your Spare Time

How to Become Financially Successful by Owning Your Own Business

How You Can Become Financially Independent by Investing In Real Estate (Revised Edition)

COURSES

Lowry Real Estate Investment Seminar

Creative Real Estate Financing

Successful Property Management

Foreclosures and Distressed Properties

Lowry Business Success Seminar

NEWSLETTERS

"Winning with Real Estate"

TELEVISION

"Fortune Builders"

HOW TO MAKE MONEY IN *REAL ESTATE* WITH GOVERNMENT LOANS AND PROGRAMS

ALBERT LOWRY

SIMON AND SCHUSTER
New York

Library of Congress Cataloging in Publication Data
Lowry, Albert J.
How to make money in real estate with government loans
and programs.

Includes index.
1. Real estate investment—United States. 2. Mortgage
loans—United States. 3. Real property tax—United
States. 4. Housing—United States—Finance. I. Title.
HD1382.5.L6797   1985   332.7'2'0937   85-8236
ISBN 0-671-55185-X

*This publication is designed to provide accurate information, not
legal advice.*

CONTENTS

Contents

CHAPTER THREE
SPECIAL PROGRAMS FOR SPECIAL PEOPLE   46

CHAPTER FOUR
ACQUIRING PROPERTIES WITH NO CASH OR CREDIT   64

CHAPTER FIVE
GETTING CASH BACK AT THE CLOSING   76

CHAPTER SIX
OPTIONS: REWARDS WITHOUT RISKS   87

CHAPTER SEVEN
YOUR CHECK REALLY *IS* IN THE MAIL 104

CHAPTER EIGHT
LOW PAYMENTS, HIGH INCOME 113

CHAPTER NINE
HOW UNCLE SAM CAN MAKE YOU WEALTHY 132

CHAPTER TEN
GOVERNMENT-OWNED REAL ESTATE FOR PENNIES ON THE DOLLAR 144

CHAPTER ELEVEN

GET BACK ALL THE TAXES YOU PAID
IN THE LAST THREE YEARS   166

CHAPTER TWELVE

REHABILITATION LOANS AND OTHER GOODIES   178

CHAPTER THIRTEEN

BILLIONS OF DOLLARS ARE WAITING FOR YOU   187

TO THE READER

If I were the so-called, proverbial "betting man," I'd start out by offering to make you a wager. But then, I only like to bet on virtually "sure things," and my experience in real estate investing obviously dictates prudence if not restraint. And yet, in talking to so many people over the years, I've come to an unwavering conclusion that you've picked up this book for one of two reasons. Maybe, for both. Either you are longingly seeking to buy your first home or second home, or else you are in pursuit of financial independence through the means of investing in real estate. Am I right in *your* case?

Let's examine the first reason for just a moment. If you've tuned in to the forecasters of doom, you've heard them repeatedly proclaim how it is now impossible for the average person to buy his or her own home as a first-time buyer. They cite such reasons as "outlandishly high prices," "zooming interest rates," and "the unrealistic, self-serving attitudes" of property-owners, politicians and the like. Even so, untold thousands of people, average people from every walk of life, many with little or no credit or even a bank account, are now realizing the fallacy of these false prophets. Indeed, these were the very same cries we heard some twenty years ago. No doubt, we'll hear them again, twenty years in the future. They'll say, "Oh, why didn't I buy some real estate way back in 1985 when it would have been so easy?"

Perhaps you've decided to read this book for the second reason—in search of a sound, totally workable investment vehicle, designed to help you build personal wealth by investing in real estate? If your quest is for either reason—or some other—read on. . . .

I'm going to show you not only *how* but *why* your own government is vitally concerned in your success, and why they will support you in your effort to buy that seemingly elusive first home to live in now, or the second one you'd like to have for your retirement years. And I'll show you how they'll help you to get started on your road to financial security by investing in real estate.

WHAT YOU SHOULD KNOW ABOUT UNCLE SAM

MEET YOUR RICH, GENEROUS UNCLE SAM

There are hundreds of government programs that give away or loan billions of dollars each year. These are not charity or welfare programs. They are part of your birthright. You do not even have to be a citizen to qualify, so you are foolish if you do not take advantage of them. Why does the government give all of this money away or loan it at interest rates far below the normal market rates if it is not charity? Because it is an excellent way to stimulate the economy in what the government considers to be socially desirable ways.

HOMEOWNERS ARE BETTER CITIZENS

A nation of homeowners is going to be happier and more productive than a nation of renters. Therefore, the government tries to encourage people to buy their own homes. But there are many people who just can't afford a home of their own, even with all the government help that is available. These people are destined to remain renters and they too need places to live. Since there is not much incentive for developers to build rental housing, particularly low- and moderate-income rental housing, the government also has programs to subsidize rents for low-income tenants and to encourage investors to build and manage rental housing. This is why real estate offers such marvelous tax benefits, especially for rental housing and other income-producing properties, but that is only the tip of a very large iceberg.

UNCLE SAM, THE REAL ESTATE TYCOON

The government is in the real estate business in a massive way. In an attempt to clean house, HUD sold 50,000 units it owned just in 1984 alone. These were government owned and managed properties. Those numbers don't begin to reflect the number of privately owned and managed housing units that are subsidized by the government in one way or another; in most areas of the country no rental housing has been built for years without the government's help.

Thousands, if not millions, have profited and are profiting every day from these programs. People have become millionaires with the help

14

and encouragement of their rich uncle, so what is stopping you? If you are like most people, what has been stopping you has been the fact that you didn't know that these programs exist. There is the true paradox: the government spends billions creating these programs but they don't get the word out to the public. All that money is sitting there for the taking but no one knows about it. . . .

Why Pay for Free Information?

But, of course, now you know . . . and many of you are probably sitting there right now asking yourselves: "Why should I buy this special book from Al Lowry just to find out about government loans and grants? I am an American citizen like anyone else. . . . Why should I pay money for that information when I can just get it myself for free?" Those of you who feel that way are absolutely right. This information is not privileged or secret. It is available to anyone. You don't have to be Al Lowry, the famous real estate expert, to get it. But you do have to have the perseverance of Sherlock Holmes to track it down unless you know what you are looking for and how to find it. I have years of experience dealing with government loan programs, but just to make sure that I was bringing you all the latest updated information available, I went to the offices of the Department of Housing and Urban Development, better known as HUD, during a recent visit to San Francisco. HUD handles most of the federal loans and grants for housing through the Federal Housing Administration (FHA) and such programs as the Section 8 Program for low-income renters. That is why I went to the HUD offices in the Federal Building at 450 Golden Gate Avenue.

A Visit to HUD

The bureaucracy being what it is, it took me a few minutes running around from one office to the next before I finally got what I was after, or part of it at any rate. The woman behind the desk gave me a thin booklet listing HUD programs. Since I knew that not nearly all the available programs were listed in that pamphlet, I asked her where I could get any information about additional HUD programs. "Well," she said, "if you go to One Embarcadero Plaza [about a mile away in the heart of the downtown traffic jam] to our other office, they have a library of HUD publications, but we don't have anything else here."

So I went to One Embarcadero Plaza (against my better judgment) and spent the next twenty minutes hunting for a parking space and then walking several blocks once I found one. I took the elevator to the sixteenth floor (not the fifteenth as the woman at 450 Golden Gate Avenue had told me) and asked the receptionist where the HUD library was located since I was researching available HUD programs. After handing me the same thin booklet I had already received, she assured me that if only I would go to the other HUD office at 450 Golden Gate Avenue, I would probably get more information since the HUD library was located there.

Fortunately, I had other sources of information and was not dependent on the bureaucracy to supply it. I was able to get the facts and make them available to you in this book. To those of you who would rather play detective and find the information on your own, I wish the best of luck.

The information is there. All you have to do is track it down and squeeze it out of the bureaucrats. For those of you who have decided to take the easy way, read on. I am confident that it will prove to be well worth your while.

CHAPTER ONE

NOW ANYONE CAN OWN A HOME

IF YOU ARE A HOMEBUYER YOU SHOULD READ THIS. It will show you many different ways to get a home with little or no down payment, at the best interest rate available. The government doesn't have programs only for renters and investors. Homebuyers are well taken care of as well. The government provides loan subsidies and guarantees to help people buy their own homes and to help builders provide housing at affordable prices.

GOVERNMENT-SUBSIDIZED BUILDERS OFFER LOWER INTEREST RATES than banks, savings and loan, and mortgage companies featuring conventional loans. They provide buyers with HUD/FHA (the Federal Housing Administration, part of the U.S. Department of Housing and Urban Development), VA (Veterans Administration), and FmHA (the Farmers Home Administration, a division of the U.S. Department of Agriculture) financing at less than the market rate of interest for conventional loans.

For example, if conventional loans are going at 13% interest per annum, then builders who are offering HUD, VA, and FmHA financing might be able to make loans available at anywhere from 10% to 12%. They can do this because the money costs them less than conventional financing would and they pass this saving on to the home-buyers.

THE GOVERNMENT MAKES IT EASY FOR BEGINNING BUYERS by guaranteeing the loans and insuring the lenders against any losses. This means that lenders don't need as large a safety cushion with government-insured loans. They can afford to accept lower down payments. This makes homeownership accessible to a much larger portion of the community. This is the government's main goal in providing loan guarantees.

But, that's not all that the government does for homebuyers. Besides helping people buy homes, the government wants to make sure that they enjoy those homes, too.

THE GOVERNMENT SETS CONSTRUCTION STANDARDS FOR INSURED HOUSING that are stricter than the normal building codes. HUD, VA, and FmHA all have their own inspectors and their own sets of standards. Whether you are buying a new house or an older one, you can be sure that if it's financed with government-insured money, it will be in excellent condition by the time you close escrow. The plumbing, wiring, heating, roof, structure, and general layout all have to conform to government-approved standards or the government won't insure the financing.

REHAB PROJECTS ARE EXCEPTIONS TO THE RULE, because it is understood that these properties are being purchased "as is" and the buyer intends to rehabilitate them. All of that is taken into account in the price and the funding. With government-owned repos, they are sold dirt cheap when all-cash bids are required. The idea is to rehab them and refinance them. With other rehab projects, purchase and rehab money are combined in one package.

There Are Many Special Programs for Homebuyers with Special Needs. No matter what you think may be stopping you from buying a home—bad credit, lack of money, lack of down payment money—the chances are that there is a government program that can help you. To find out what programs can help you, you have to know what programs are available. So we're going to look at various programs and see how they can be used for your benefit.

FHA Homebuyer Loans are available to almost anyone. When we talk about government programs to benefit homebuyers, the only logical place to start is with the FHA (the Federal Housing Administration) a division of the Department of Housing and Urban Development, since FHA programs are the most numerous and the best known of all the government programs for homebuyers. There are other FHA programs for investors and there are lots of other government programs for homebuyers but we will get into those later.

The FHA has been criticized repeatedly over the years for a variety of reasons: It is bureaucratic. It is inefficient. It only works in certain areas and benefits the middle class. It doesn't really do anything for the poor. All of these things are true and yet FHA loans have put a generation of buyers into their first homes and, in many cases, their second homes and even their third. Many builders would not be in business if they could not get FHA financing to help them sell the homes that they build.

The real problem is that people expect FHA loans to be too many things to too many people. That is why we are going to look at what they are, what they do, and how you can use them to make money.

WHAT ARE FHA LOANS? They are loans guaranteed by the federal government to enable people to buy homes. They are not for the poor. They are meant to benefit the middle and working classes, the people who can afford to buy their own homes, but not without some help. They can't afford 10% or 20% down.

These are the people who keep our economy going. When they buy houses, it creates jobs and a tax base for their communities. The country as a whole benefits. There are other programs for the poor and we will get into those later, but the basic FHA mortgage assistance programs do not fall into that category and so no one has to feel ashamed or as if he is taking advantage of the public's generosity by participating in any of these programs.

Actually, the government doesn't usually even lend money. All it does is to guarantee loans made by private lenders. This means that people can borrow more money with less security because the government guarantees to make good on the loan if they default. This is what makes FHA loan programs so popular: people can get in with a low down payment. Let's look at a typical situation to see how it would actually work.

BOB AND BETTY BLUECOLLAR WANT TO BUY A HOME. Bob works at a steady job and earns a good but not spectacular income, while Betty stays home and takes care of Bob Jr. and little Emily. They try to save money, but it's hard. They have a little money in the bank, but not much. Now they are determined to own a home of their own.

One day, Bob and Betty finally decide to act on their dream. They go to see a real estate broker and they tell her that they want to buy a house. She says, "Fine," and then sits them down for a little talk on finances. She wants to find out if they qualify for a loan to buy a house and what price range they can really afford, so she starts asking a lot of questions about where Bob works and how long he has been employed there and how much money he makes. Then, once she has all this information, she tells Bob and Betty that they can qualify for a loan of about $50,000. This puts them in a fairly good position, since it means that they should be able to afford a $60,000 house and the range of prices in their area is between $45,000 and $70,000. Naturally, Bob and Betty are happy to hear this and they immediately go out with the agent to see what is available.

Although they would prefer four bedrooms, they soon come to the conclusion that they will probably have to settle for three bedrooms if they want to keep the price at $60,000 or less. They don't see anything they like, but ask the broker to keep looking and give them a call when she sees anything interesting. She calls them a few times over the course of the next several weeks and they look at about a dozen houses before they finally find one that they are really excited about. The seller is asking $63,000, but the agent is confident that he will accept a little bit less, so Bob and Betty make an offer for $59,000 and, sure enough, they get it accepted.

BOB AND BETTY APPLY FOR A CONVENTIONAL LOAN. Now the fun starts. Their broker has them fill out a loan application and she submits it to a local bank or savings and loan. The purchase contract gives Bob and Betty up to four weeks to get the loan and then another week to close the deal, so now the waiting begins. The broker assures them that their application should be approved and that it will probably be less than four weeks—ideally about two—before they get a definite answer. In the meantime they have to take one form to their bank to verify the amount of money in their account and another one to Bob's employer to verify his income. Until those come back, the lender won't even actually begin to evaluate their application.

Bob takes the Verification of Employment form to his supervisor at work and then takes the Verification of Deposit form to the bank. Everything is looking rosy. Then, a week and a half later, they get a happy call from their broker. The loan has been approved. They will be getting a formal statement from the bank in a couple of days.

Sure enough, in two days a letter arrives from the bank stating that Bob and Betty have been formally approved for a $50,000 loan. The letter tells them how much the interest rate will be and what loan fees, or points, the bank will be charging in connection with the loan and what the approximate amount of the other closing costs should be. The loan fee will be equal to 2.5% of the loan amount ($1,250) and the other closing costs should come to approximately another $1,000. This means that Bob and Betty will have to come up with approximately $11,250 at the close of escrow. This will just about wipe out their savings, but it will be well worth it because now they will own their own home. The payments on their loan will be approximately $515 a month and taxes and insurance should be about another $100 a month, so their budget will not be overly strained.

This story has a happy ending. Bob and Betty were able to qualify for a conventional loan and get the house that they wanted with conventional, non-government-guaranteed financing. They did not have to turn to FHA financing. But now let's change their situation just a bit and see what happens.

BOB AND BETTY SEEK LOW DOWN PAYMENT FINANCING. Let's say that Bob and Betty did not have $11,000 in the bank. They can still afford the monthly payments but coming up with the down payment is just more than they can handle. Even if they can come up with the extra money that they need by borrowing it, the bank might not be willing to give them the $50,000 mortgage that they need because they cannot show the money for the down payment in their bank account.

Naturally enough, they are upset to hear this, but they still want the house. They ask their broker for any alternative suggestions: Isn't there any way that she can think of that they might be able to get the house without having to come up with all that cash?

A LOAN FROM THE SELLER is one way to solve the problem. "Yes," the broker tells them, there are several ways that they can possibly get the house without having to put up all that cash. They can try to get the seller to carry a second mortgage for the balance of the down payment, the difference between the amount of cash that they can comfortably spare and the amount that they need for the down payment and the closing costs.

BOB AND BETTY CONSIDER A 90% OR 95% LOAN. This is one possible way to do things. If they feel uncomfortable with that idea, or the seller won't cooperate, they can then try to get a 90% loan that would require only a 10% down payment. The only problem is that 90% loans are slightly harder to qualify for and lenders charge more money for a 90% loan. For example, the interest rate would be 12.5% instead of 12% and there would be a loan fee of 3% instead of 2.5%, so it would cost them about $250 more up front and another $20 a month or so for the added interest.

BOB AND BETTY CONSIDER AN FHA LOAN. That would only require a down payment of 3% of the first $25,000 of the purchase price, 5% of the next $25,000, and 10% of the balance. In Bob and Betty's case, this means that they would have to put up a total of $2,900 (3% of $25,000 is $750, plus 5% of the next $25,000, or $1,250, plus 10% of the final $9,000). By law, they would pay only one point for their loan, so their loan fee would be only $560.

Naturally, Bob and Betty decide to go for the FHA loan. After all, with terms like that it is a much better deal. But then the broker throws in the bad news: They can't even apply for the FHA loan unless the seller agrees.

Why would the seller disagree? Bob and Betty wonder. Why would he even care? After all, he will not only be getting the house sold, but he will be getting all cash as well. Under those circumstances, it shouldn't matter to him what kind of loan Bob and Betty get.

FHA DILEMMA: BUYERS' DELIGHT, SELLER'S BAD NEWS. This is when the broker tells them the bad news about FHA loans. First of all, there is the waiting time. It takes anywhere from two to four months to get an FHA loan approved and funded. With a conventional loan you can get the money and close escrow in four to six weeks and you can get loan approval—so that the seller at least knows that the deal is going to happen—within two to three weeks. This delay is the first thing that most sellers object to. Unfortunately, it is not the only thing.

The next thing that most sellers object to about FHA loans is the fact that the buyers are allowed to pay only one point. Why do sellers object to this? Because it means that whenever the lender is charging more than one point—which is most of the time—the sellers have to pay the difference. Naturally enough, this doesn't sit too well with sellers. They don't like it and most of them will accept those terms only if they are desperate or if they think that they can raise the sales price to cover the points; naturally Bob and Betty are not anxious to renegotiate and wind up paying a higher price for the house.

Then there is the inspection and appraisal, the broker explains. The house must be approved by the FHA inspectors as being up to FHA standards and the price must match the value put upon the property by the FHA appraisers. The seller has to approve before either the appraisal or the inspection can be done.

Bob and Betty look at each other. None of that sounds too bad. They will have the house inspected so that they know that it is in good shape and they will get it appraised so that they know that they are getting a good deal. Heck, if the seller is afraid of an inspection or an appraisal, then they probably do not really want the house anyway.

So the broker goes back to the seller or the seller's agent and explains the situation. What happens next depends upon how much the seller knows about FHA financing, how anxious he is to sell, and what condition the house is in.

If the seller and his agent don't know much about FHA financing, then the seller will probably accept the change as long as he can raise the price enough to cover the cost of the points. As long as he comes out netting the same amount of money in the end, the seller probably will not object too strongly.

On the other hand, a seller who is familiar with FHA financing will insist that he will accept the new terms only if the contract is contingent upon his, the seller's, approval of the FHA inspection and appraisal report. That way he will not get stuck making unnecessary repairs and improvements or lowering the price because the appraisal came in low.

Using FHA Rules to Your Own Advantage as a Buyer

What does this mean to you as a buyer? How can you use it to make money in real estate? It's very simple. If you can get a seller to sell you a house and agree to take FHA financing without any contingencies, then you can get him to do all the repairs for you. You can buy a house in poor condition at rock-bottom prices and then have the seller put it in tip-top shape before the close of escrow. If the appraisal comes in low and there is no contingency in the contract to cover that, then you can force the seller to sell you the house at the appraised price rather than the previously agreed upon purchase price. You can sometimes pick up thousands of dollars in free equity this way. You are not cheating anyone or doing anything underhanded, you are just sticking to a strict interpretation of FHA rules. It should be up to the seller to know exactly what those rules are and how they will affect him. It is not your responsibility to interpret those rules for him.

Even if you don't save any money, at least you know that you are getting a house that is in excellent condition by the time that you close escrow. You will also know that you are not overpaying for it, because you will have a report from a professional appraiser telling you the true value of the property.

FHA ASSUMABLE GOLD MINE

That is just the beginning. The best part is yet to come. The FHA loan you get today could well turn into a gold mine when you get ready to sell the property. Why? Because FHA loans are automatically assumable, at the existing interest rate, for just a small fee (usually under $100) to the lender.

Picture yourself in this position: You get a loan today at 12.5% interest. In five years when you want to sell the property, interest rates on new mortgage loans are 17% to 18% and money is tight even at those rates. Do you think you will have much trouble selling a house with a fully assumable 12.5% loan?

Remember the last time you saw this happen? From about 1980 to 1982, people with assumable loans were getting thousands of dollars more for their houses. Sellers who could not offer buyers help with financing were suddenly known as distressed sellers. They were distressed by the fact that they could not sell their houses except at bargain basement prices. The people with older low-interest FHA loans were able to sell their houses for high prices or "wrap" the existing loans—offer to carry overriding mortgages (or deeds of trust) at a slightly higher interest rate—and get a nice little income each month.

But what if the seller that you are dealing with is familiar with FHA financing and doesn't want to give away thousands of dollars in free equity, points, and possible repairs and improvements? Then it will probably come down to the area where the house is located or how motivated the seller really is.

The seller's motivation, or lack of it, is, of course, hard to predict in advance. Each seller is different and will react slightly differently to the same situation. But the location is another matter. There are certain areas that are FHA areas, meaning that many if not most homes in the area are financed with FHA financing because the buyers often do not have the resources for a conventional down payment of 10% or 20%.

FHA Areas and Non-FHA Areas

Other areas are more affluent, more desirable. They attract buyers who are willing and able to come up with a conventional down payment. In areas like that it is usually difficult to get sellers to accept FHA financing. Why should they put up with all the bureaucracy and inconvenience and expense if they don't have to? It should not be difficult to find out where the FHA areas are in your city, town, county or region. The price range will tell you a lot, and so will the type of people who live there. As I said before, the people who use FHA financing are generally working class, moderate income, family people. Their houses are not very expensive because FHA puts a ceiling on the amount that anyone can pay for their home if they want to qualify for FHA financing.

In most locations, FHA will not finance any home being purchased for more than $68,500; but in certain areas (such as San Francisco) that have been designated special higher-priced areas where this limit is impractical, the purchase price can be up to $90,000. This generally excludes the more expensive homes in any area, and in some areas even the $90,000 limit excludes many. This is why I say there are FHA areas and non-FHA areas; it should be simple enough to learn which are which in the area where you live.

If you are in an area where it is a strong sellers' market and homes generally sell quickly and easily, then most sellers feel they have no reason to accept FHA financing. If on the other hand it is a buyers' market, where properties do not sell that quickly or easily and buyers are reluctant to put up 20% or even 10% of the purchase price as a down payment, then FHA financing will have more of an appeal for sellers.

FHA Financing and New Homes

The other big market, perhaps the biggest market for FHA financing, is among buyers of new tract homes. It doesn't matter whether it is a buyers' market or a sellers' market. Unless you are looking at luxury homes beyond the FHA price range, the majority of new developments offer FHA financing, often at below market interest rates. The reason for this is that builders want to move homes, a lot of homes, and they know that they must offer attractive financing in order to do it efficiently. A homeowner with one house to sell can often afford to wait for the right buyer to come along. The builder with two or three hundred houses to sell is in quite a different position.

The builders also have an advantage or two that homeowners don't have. First of all, the builders know that they have to build to FHA standards. Therefore, it is no problem for them to pass the FHA inspection. They also know that they have to keep the price within the FHA-approved limits, so they have no trouble with the FHA appraisals, and finally, the builders can "buy down" the interest rate, in order to make their homes more competitive in the marketplace. The builders are able to do this by paying the lenders a premium, a lump sum of cash up front, in exchange for a lower interest rate on the financing. For example, they may pay $2,000 a house to lower the interest rate by 1%, $4,000 a house to lower it by 2%, etc.

Of course, the cost of the "buy-down" is usually passed right along to the buyers, by asking higher prices for the homes, but most buyers don't even think about that. They just know that they are getting a lower interest rate than they would normally get if they bought an older home.

Private parties selling their own homes don't usually have these advantages. First of all, FHA financing programs only began in 1934, so many older homes were not built to FHA standards and it would cost too much to bring them up to FHA standards without adding substantially to the value of the house. Until recently it was difficult if not impossible to buy down the interest rate on a loan unless you had the money to buy up a block of loans—two or three hundred or more—the way the builders did it. This has changed in the last couple of years, but most private parties still are not really aware of all the options available.

Finally, there is the matter of appraisals versus the asking price. The FHA seldom questions the price put on new tract homes. As long as they are priced within the FHA limits, the builder should not have any trouble getting the financing approved. The same is, of course, not true for one-time sales of older homes by private individuals. The asking price may be well above the FHA appraiser's value.

These are some of the problems and pitfalls that Bob and Betty can expect to face. None of them are insurmountable. They can be overcome if Bob and Betty are really determined to get the house and the seller is equally determined to sell it. But they do exist and they do represent the dark side of FHA financing and that is why I want you to be aware of them. But now that we have talked a little about the basic FHA homeowner's loan program and what it does right and what it does wrong, let's talk a little bit about exactly what it is and how it works.

How FHA Loan Guarantees Work

As I previously stated, the FHA does not actually loan money. What it does is guarantee loans made by private lenders, usually mortgage companies. These mortgage companies get the money to loan out in two ways. First of all, they have investors who put up money to invest in mortgages. These can be wealthy individuals who put up a lot of money and finance one or more mortgages all by themselves, or they can be people with only modest sums to invest, say five to ten thousand dollars, which is then put into a mortgage pool, which means that the money from several of these small investors will be put together to finance one mortgage. This is one way that it is done.

THE GOVERNMENT NATIONAL MORTGAGE ASSOCIATION ("GINNIE MAE")

The other way is through what is known as mortgage-based securities issued through a company known as the Government National Mortgage Association or GNMA, better known as "Ginnie Mae." Ginnie Mae is actually a semi-private company set up by the federal government to keep mortgage money available to fund FHA and VA (Veterans Administration) loans. Ginnie Mae buys up millions of these loans from the mortgage brokers who make them and then issues securities backed by pools of mortgages, which are sold on the stock exchange just like stocks and bonds.

The FHA's role in all this is to guarantee those loans. If the borrower defaults on an FHA loan, then the mortgage broker can go to the FHA and ask them to take over the loan and reimburse him or his clients for the money that they have invested. FHA then takes over the loan and tries to collect from the borrower.

This offers borrowers another advantage over conventional loans. If they get into financial trouble through no fault of their own, such as losing their job or falling ill, they can petition FHA for a moratorium on the payments and save their home from foreclosure. If, however, the borrower has no good excuse for falling behind in his payments and fails to clear up the default, then FHA takes the house, just the way any other lender would do under the circumstances.

Actually, FHA does not even guarantee the entire loan, just 25% of it. But this is enough to insure that even if the appraisal was wrong and the property cannot be resold for the entire loan amount the investors and the mortgage broker will be covered and will not lose any money.

The Lender's Security Blanket

If Bob and Betty wanted to buy a house with conventional financing, they would have to put down between $6,000 and $12,000 as their real estate broker explained to them. This is the lender's security blanket. He knows that Bob and Betty have a real stake in the house. If things get rough for them economically, they are not just going to pick up and walk away because they then would lose their down payment. The lender also knows that even if they do walk away from the house, he can get his money back by selling it to someone else.

He doesn't have to sell the house for $60,000 to get his money back. He only has to sell it for the amount of the loan ($48,000 to $54,000). Assuming that the house is really worth approximately $60,000, this gives the lender a nice little cushion to fall back on.

With FHA loans, the lender doesn't have this sort of cushion. Remember, Bob and Betty only had to put up $2,900 for their down payment and then they were able to borrow $57,100. This does not provide much of a cushion for the lender. If he had to foreclose he might have a hard time getting back the full amount of the loan. This is why the FHA guarantees up to 25% of it. If Bob and Betty default, the FHA will pay the lender up to $14,275 to compensate him for any possible loss on the resale of the property. Or FHA will make good on the entire loan and take over the property at the lender's request. In practice, this is what usually happens in such situations.

Naturally, FHA is assuming a certain amount of risk this way, but there are safeguards. These are loans, not grants, and applicants are screened at least as carefully as they would be if they were applying for conventional loans instead. Applicants must have good credit and employment histories and, generally, their proposed payments cannot exceed 25% of their gross income. If they meet all the other requirements except this one, they can apply for a graduated payment loan instead, which will be discussed in detail later.

PRIVATE MORTGAGE INSURANCE

Applicants are also required to pay for private mortgage insurance to back up the FHA guarantee. Known as PMI, this generally adds between .25% and .5% to the interest rate. If the interest rate on their FHA loan is 12% per annum, then Bob and Betty's payments will be equal to the payments on a loan with an interest rate of 12.25% or 12.5%, without any PMI required. Once Bob and Betty have paid off at least 20% of the principal balance of the loan, several years down the road, they can request that the PMI be dropped and their payments lowered accordingly.

WHO IS ELIGIBLE FOR FHA LOANS?

Anyone who is a legal resident of the United States and over eighteen years old can apply for an FHA loan. There are no special requirements and you don't even have to be a citizen. If you are interested in pursuing it, either call or visit your local HUD office or find a local lender who handles FHA loans and get an application.

What Does the Mortgage Broker Do?

The mortgage broker is the lender most likely to be handling FHA loans in your area. A few banks and savings and loan associations also handle them. Since they are set up to handle conventional loans, most of them leave FHA and VA loans to the mortgage brokers, who are specifically set up to deal with them. They are prepared to handle all the special FHA paperwork and they are in contact with FHA-approved appraisers, etc. They are really the FHA's field agents, the front-line troops who deal directly with the public.

The FHA is not set up to do this on its own. It is set up as a guarantor and overseer of loans, not as a direct lender. The FHA's job is to set the requirements and standards for the loan program, rather than to deal with the public on a one-to-one basis. The FHA reviews all the paperwork, hires and trains the inspectors, and certifies lenders and appraisers to participate in its various programs. The mortgage broker does just about all the rest.

The broker is the middle man between the investors who put up money for loans, the borrowers who want that money to buy homes, and the FHA, which guarantees the loans so that the borrowers can get away with putting up only a small down payment. The broker finds the investors. He finds the borrowers. He takes the initial application and then forwards it to the FHA's local office. He also arranges the appraisals and credit checks, and he qualifies the borrower.

How Mortgage Brokers Get Paid

All of this is a lot of work and mortgage brokers do not work for free. They collect a fee every time a borrower receives a loan. This is where the points or loan fees go. Sometimes, the mortgage broker gets to keep the entire fee; other times, he has to split it with the investors to make the loan a more attractive investment if the interest rate is not high enough, but this is his sole means of compensation. The interest the borrower pays goes only to the investors who put up the money.

Well then, can't you just bypass the mortgage broker entirely and save that loan fee or at least part of it? No, because as we saw earlier, the FHA is not set up to be a direct lender or to deal with the public. You have to work through a mortgage broker or some other type of lender and you have to pay points. Or, rather, you have to convince the seller to pay them. There is really no way to get around it.

FHA Interest Rate Ceiling

Until recently, the amount of points that the seller had to pay could vary wildly, depending on the FHA interest rate at the time. If the interest rate went up, then the points usually went down. But if the interest rate remained the same, or went down in times of change, then the points were usually raised accordingly. This was because FHA interest rates were not free to float up or down with the market. The interest rate on conventional loans has always been free to seek its own level, with each lender setting his own rate and then moving that rate up or

down as the times demanded. But FHA interest rates were set by the
Secretary of Housing and Urban Development. This often caused a situation where FHA interest rates were below the average rate for conventional loans but the points on FHA loans were prohibitively high
Naturally, this pleased buyers but scared off sellers. It made it hard to
get sellers to accept FHA loans. The way it worked was like this: One
day the rate for FHA loans would be set at 10%, which would be just
about the average rate for conventional loans as well. This means that
the points the mortgage brokers were charging would be relatively low,
usually 2% to 3% of the loan amount. This would be just the amount
that they charge for their own services. None of it would go to the investors since they would make their money on the interest. The
amount of points charged would vary from lender to lender, since they
were free to set the points at any level they liked. Only the interest rate
was regulated. Periodically, the money supply would tighten up and
interest rates on conventional loans would go up, but FHA interest
rates would stay the same, until the HUD secretary decided to raise
them. Until that happened, there would be an interest rate gap between FHA and conventional loans. In order to bridge this gap and
make FHA loans a more attractive investment, the mortgage brokers
would start charging 6% to 8% of the loan amount in points. They
would continue to take their 2% to 3% fee for putting the loans together
and the rest would go to the investors who put up the money for the
loans.

FHA Interest Rate Ceiling Abolished

Now all of that has changed. Secretary of Housing and Urban Development Samuel Pierce decided to abolish the interest rate ceiling for
FHA loans at the end of 1983, so that each lender could set his own

interest rates, just as he sets his own loan fees or points. The idea was to stabilize the market for FHA loans by eliminating prohibitively high points. This makes FHA financing even more accessible to even more buyers.

That about sums up what there is to say about FHA's general homeowner's loan program. Now it's time to talk about getting flexible and shaping your loan to fit your lifestyle.

KEY POINTS TO REMEMBER

1. Conventional loans are not insured by the government.
2. FHA homebuyer loans are available to just about anyone.
3. The FHA has strict inspection standards.
4. FHA loans require less down payment money than conventional loans.
5. The FHA has strict price limits that exclude expensive homes.
6. FHA loans are fully assumable.

CHAPTER TWO

FLEXIBLE PROGRAMS FOR FLEXIBLE LIFESTYLES

THE GRADUATED PAYMENT LOAN

The graduated payment loan (FHA 245 Program) is designed for people who expect their income to go up in the future. They start off paying a little less than they would with a normal FHA loan, and then their payments gradually go up over a period of years until those payments are slightly higher than they would normally be; then they level off and remain fixed for the remainder of the loan period. There are five different options, each one (in theory) featuring a different time period during which the loan payments gradually increase. The time periods range from three years to ten years, but in practice, there is one plan that most lenders actually use. This gives the borrower five years to increase his income. Payments start out lower than they would normally be for the loan amount and interest rate involved and the borrower is allowed to qualify on the basis of these artificially low payments. This, of course, makes it easier for the borrower to get the loan. The second year, the payments increase. They continue to increase the third year, the fourth year, and the fifth year. Finally, in the sixth year, they level out at a point slightly higher than they would normally be for a fixed-rate loan and remain at that level for the remaining 25 years of the 30-year loan term.

In other words, let's say that Bob and Betty were getting a normal FHA fixed-rate loan for $55,000 at 12% interest. Their payments would be approximately $565 a month and they would have to show a gross income of over $2,000 a month to qualify. If they decided to get a graduated payment loan instead, they might start out with payments of only $450 a month the first year. This means they would only need an income of approximately $1,800 a month to qualify. Clearly, this would make things much easier for them, but, if their income did not go up enough, they could be in trouble later, because their payments definitely will go up, whether they can handle the increase or not.

This is necessary in order to make up the deficit—the difference between what their payments should have been and what they actually were. At the end of the first year, there would be a payment deficit of $1,380 ($115 a month—the difference between $450 and $565, times 12 months). But, even in the second year, the payments still are not going to be $565 a month. They will probably be about $475 a month, so that by the end of the second year there will be an even bigger deficit.

The third year, the payments will probably go up to about $500 a month, the fourth year to about $525, the fifth year to $550 or $560 a month, and then in the sixth year they will probably go up to about $590 or $600 a month and remain at that level for the remainder of the loan term. This will make up for the deficit and in the long run provide the lender with a little extra profit (and therefore, some incentive for making graduated payment loans in the first place).

For young families starting out, people who have recently started a business, or anyone who has a relatively low income now but expects it to go up in the future, this program provides the flexibility that can mean the difference between getting the house they want today and having to wait until some time in the future.

CONDOMINIUM HOUSING

Condominium housing (Section 234) is another option that Bob and Betty can take advantage of. In addition to providing insurance guarantees on loans for single-family homes and owner-occupied apartment complexes of up to four units, FHA also provides for people who want to own their own condominiums. This is done under Section 234(c) of the Housing Act. A condominium is defined as joint ownership of common areas and facilities by the separate owners in the project. Projects must contain at least four units, but they may be detached, semi-detached, row, walkup, or high-rise elevator buildings. Any credit-worthy person may apply for a mortgage under this program.

This could be just the program that Bob and Betty need, if they live in an area where there is an abundance of apartment buildings but few single-family houses. It allows apartment dwellers to enjoy the privileges and pleasures of homeownership. In recent years, condominiums have become increasingly popular in urban areas. Building owners get increased profits by selling individual units and buyers get appreciation and tax benefits.

Manufactured (Mobile) Homes (Title I)

In order to help provide low-cost alternative financing for those who cannot afford traditional homes, FHA also insures loans for the purchase of manufactured or mobile homes. Anyone able to make the cash investment and the mortgage payments may apply for a Title I loan for up to $22,500 ($35,000 if two or more modules are being financed). The maximum repayment schedule is 20 years and 32 days.

Again, this program offers appreciation and tax benefits to people who might otherwise never be able to afford a home of their own. It is also popular with retirees who want to scale down their lifestyles to conform with their limited budgets. Many of them sell their traditional homes, buy a mobile home with part of the proceeds, and then use the rest to supplement their pensions, social security, etc.

Cooperative Housing (Section 213)

If you are a member of a nonprofit housing cooperative or plan to be, then there is a loan program for you too. HUD insures loans by private lenders on cooperative housing projects of five or more units. The units must be occupied by members of nonprofit cooperative housing ownership corporations and the loans may be used to finance new contruction, acquisition, rehabilitation, improvement or repair of a project already owned, and resale of individual memberships.

Loans made under this program may also be used for construction of projects composed of individual family dwellings—to be bought by individual members with separate insured mortgages—so the definition of cooperative housing is a fairly liberal one.

Who is eligible to apply? Nonprofit corporations or trusts organized to construct homes for members of the corporation or beneficiaries of the trust; and qualified sponsors who intend to sell the projects to nonprofit corporations or trusts.

In other words, you could get together with four friends, relatives, neighbors, people you work with, or whoever, form your own nonprofit corporation, and apply for a cooperative housing loan. You would not even have to live in the same building or share the responsibilities of having a common mortgage. As long as there are at least five units involved and your corporation is nonprofit, then you can even buy separate houses and have separate mortgages. Remember, nonprofit does not have to mean low-income housing and it does not have to mean that you are in business to help anyone but yourselves. As long as there are no stockholders in your corporation who will be collecting dividends or making a profit in any way, you can qualify for this program. Its purpose is not necessarily to help the poor, but just to encourage and facilitate the development of nonprofit cooperative housing ventures.

FINAL OVERVIEW OF GOVERNMENT HOMEOWNER PROGRAMS

Let's go through a quick rundown on what we have already covered. Let's go back to our friends Bob and Betty and follow their progress as they work their way through the available programs, starting with the basic, fixed-payment conventional loan, trying to find the one that will suit them best.

1) Conventional Loans

These are not subsidized or insured by the government in any way. If Bob and Betty want to buy a $60,000 house, they will have to put down between $6,000 and $12,000, plus closing costs, for a total of $8,000 to $14,000 in cash. It will take anywhere from four to six weeks to close escrow and two to three weeks to get loan approval. They will have to have good employment and credit histories and their monthly income before taxes and expenses will have to be at least three and a half to four times the amount of their proposed monthly payments. They can expect to pay a loan fee equal to 1% to 3% of the loan amount and they are more or less on their own, as far as getting the property inspected and appraised are concerned. The lender will have the property appraised, but unless it is outrageously overpriced, the lender is not likely to turn down the loan on that basis. As far as the condition of the property is concerned, the only inspection the lender is likely to require is a pest control clearance, rather than a full structural inspection.

2) FHA Homeowner Loans (Section 203(b) and (i))

This is the basic FHA homeowners loan program that is open to just about everyone. If Bob and Betty decide to use this program to buy their $60,000 house, they will only have to put down $2,900 in cash. They will pay a loan fee of not more than 1% of the loan amount, but then the seller will also have to pay anywhere from 1% to 9% of the loan amount—depending upon the current interest-rate gap, if any, between conventional and FHA loans.

The property must pass a rigorous FHA inspection before the loan is approved and the sales price must agree with the FHA appraisal. The whole process will take eight to twelve weeks before the loan can close escrow and about six weeks for loan approval. Bob and Betty still have to have good credit and employment histories and their income should be at least four times the amount of their proposed monthly payments. But, if they run into financial trouble in the future, through no fault of their own—e.g., Bob loses his job, or one of them gets sick, or something like that—they can ask FHA to take over the mortgage; if FHA agrees, they can get special repayment terms until they get back on their feet.

3) FHA Condominium Housing Loans (Section 234)

This is the program that Bob and Betty would take part in if they decided to buy a condominium instead of a single-family house or an owner-occupied apartment building of four units or less. The rules are basically the same as they would be for the Section 203(b) and (i) program, except that the unit that Bob and Betty select must be one of at least four units in order to qualify. Their down payment would be the same, assuming that they are buying a $60,000 condominium, but they would need a slightly higher income to qualify, because the condominium association fees would raise the amount of their total monthly payments.

4) FHA Graduated Payment Loans (Section 245)

This is the program that Bob and Betty would apply for if they had trouble qualifying for the loan they wanted but expected their income to go up in the future. Theoretically, there would be five different options available to them as far as payments are concerned, five different plans where their payments on their $60,000 property would start by being lower than normal (and they could qualify on the basis of those lower payments), and would then increase over the next several years until they finally level off at a point slightly higher than normal.

In practice, there is only one plan that most lenders will go along with, and that is the one where the payments increase gradually over the first five years until they level off in the sixth year and then remain fixed for the remainder of the loan term. This plan is dependent on the idea that Bob and Betty's income will go up each year for the next five years, enabling them to meet the growing payments.

5) Farmers Home Administration Homeownership Loans

This is the program that Bob and Betty might want to apply for if they live in a town or rural area of less than 20,000 people. If they qualify for this Department of Agriculture program, they can bypass the FHA entirely and not even have to put down any money at all. They can use the money to buy or build a new home, or buy and fix up an older home. Nor do they have to be farmers, or poor, to qualify. They just have to live in a rural area and be low or moderate income, as determined by the local

FmHA county supervisor. If they get the loan, they can take up to 33 years to pay it back.

6) Manufactured (Mobile) Home (Title I)

Assuming that Bob and Betty decide that a single-family home or condominium is beyond their reach for one reason or another or that it is just more than they really want to take on, then this program might provide an alternative. It would allow them to get HUD insurance for a mobile or manufactured home instead.

Since the cost of mobile homes is less than the cost of traditional single-family homes, the maximum loan amount that they could get is also less. Assuming that they qualify, they can borrow up to $22,500 if they are buying just one module, and up to $35,000 if they are buying two or more modules. They will not be able to get a 30-year loan, but instead will have to repay it within 20 years and 32 days.

7) Cooperative Housing (Section 213)

If none of the programs that we have mentioned so far work for Bob and Betty, they still have one more chance. If they get together with at least four other families, they can form their own nonprofit housing cooperative. Together they can apply for a loan (or loans) to buy or build housing for themselves or to repair and rehabilitate property they already own. They can even buy separate houses and request separate mortgages as long as they are a nonprofit cooperative housing corporation or trust organized to construct homes for members of the corporation or trust. The government won't make them a direct loan (unless they are in a rural area, in which case they should check with FmHA as opposed to FHA), but will insure a loan made to them by a private lender.

This list completes the alternatives available to Bob and Betty if they are just ordinary homebuyers seeking government assistance in buying a home. Now, let's go on to look at some of the programs available to them if they fit into any of the special categories of homebuyers that the government recognizes and deals with in special ways.

KEY POINTS TO REMEMBER

1. **Graduated payment loans make it easier for buyers to qualify.**
2. **The payments start out lower than normal and gradually rise.**
3. **Condominium loans allow apartment dwellers to become homeowners.**
4. **Mobile-home loans are also available through the FHA.**
5. **Cooperative loans are available to nonprofit groups.**
6. **Cooperative loans can be used to buy or build individual homes.**

CHAPTER THREE

SPECIAL PROGRAMS FOR SPECIAL PEOPLE

A VETERAN IS REWARDED FOR SERVICES RENDERED to his country. This may seem like a gift from heaven, but it's not. If you are a qualified veteran, this is just one of the benefits you're entitled to. It's not charity. You earned it. This is your just reward. The government wants to help you get ahead in civilian life by putting you into a home of your own.

You can get in with no money down and you will probably get a favorable interest rate as well. The government will see to it that you get a good property too, at a good price. The Veterans Administration won't let you buy just any old overpriced piece of junk.

THE GOVERNMENT PROTECTS VETERANS WHEN THEY BUY A HOME. Lenders, brokers, appraisers, builders, and anyone else who is involved with VA financed housing must be VA approved. The VA uses its own list of VA-approved appraisers to make sure the property is priced right and its own staff inspectors to make sure the property is in good condition. If the property doesn't pass VA approval, the sale won't be funded.

The VA sets its own standards for construction, above and beyond the requirements of the normal building codes. Both new homes and existing ones must meet these standards in order to qualify for VA financing. The rules even require the seller to pay most of the closing costs. All of this is nice, but to most veterans what's really important is the special terms you get with VA financing and the fact that you don't need a lot of cash.

Veterans Administration Loans

Qualified veterans who served in World War II or later can get loans of up to $135,000 with no down payment at all. This is probably the largest of the government programs that is restricted to a special group rather than being available to the public-at-large. It is not administered by the Federal Housing Administration or any other division of HUD, but by the Veterans Administration.

Basically though, it works the same way as the FHA programs. Prospective borrowers apply to a private lender, usually a mortgage broker. He lender-qualifies them, arranges for the appraisal, and then sends all the paperwork to the Veterans Administration. The property must pass an inspection and be appraised for at least the amount of the purchase price before the Veterans Administration will approve the loan. The veteran must also have a certificate of eligibility, stating that he qualifies for a VA loan and the amount he is eligible to borrow.

VA ELIGIBILITY

Qualified veterans have an eligibility of up to $135,000 to start. This means they can borrow up to $135,000 without any down payment at all. Of course, they must be able to qualify for a $135,000 loan in terms of income, employment, credit history, etc. Not every veteran can walk into a mortgage broker's office and walk out with a loan for $135,000. He or she must prove a realistic ability to make the payments. Qualifications are strict. Like the FHA homeowner's loan programs, this is not charity.

The Veterans Administration does not make the loans. It just guarantees them by promising to be responsible for up to 25% of the loan amount if the veteran should default, so borrowers are screened carefully. Just as for applicants for FHA loans, they generally must have a monthly income at least four times as great as their proposed monthly payments.

HOW MUCH CAN VETERANS BORROW?

There is another twist to VA loans. Veterans can only borrow up to the level of their remaining eligibility. Once they have used all or part of that eligibility, they cannot borrow more until it has been restored. As I said earlier, each qualified veteran starts off with a maximum eligibility of $135,000. This is the maximum amount that he can borrow without a down payment.

Once he borrows all or part of this amount, it reduces his eligibility accordingly. For example, if a qualified veteran with full eligibility borrows $50,000 to buy a home, he will have only $85,000 worth of eligibility left. If he decides to sell the home and buy another one, also using VA financing, the maximum loan he will qualify for is $85,000. The only way he can restore his full eligibility of $135,000 is to sell the home to another qualified veteran who will use his own eligibility, or cash out and pay off the loan. If he lets anyone other than a qualified veteran take over his loan, then the loan amount ($50,000) is deducted from his remaining eligibility until the loan is eventually paid off.

Many people do not realize that a veteran who has used up only part of his eligibility can qualify for a new loan up to the limit of his remaining eligibility even before the first loan is paid off. He can, but only if the first property has been sold and someone else has assumed the loan. A veteran cannot have two VA loans at once because the property must be owner-occupied in order to qualify.

Why the VA Has Tightened Its Rules

As with FHA loans, it can be up to four units, but at least one of the units must be occupied by the veteran as his primary residence. It used to be fairly easy to get around this requirement. A person could move into a property by throwing a sleeping bag on the floor and staying there for a few days and then move out and announce he had decided he did not like living there.

Now the VA has gotten stricter, so mortgage brokers generally advise living in the property for at least six months to a year before attempting to move out and get a new owner-occupied loan. But where there is a will, there is usually a way.

My favorite true story involves an unmarried couple who bought a property together using his VA eligibility. It cost only $65,000, so he still had $70,000 worth of eligibility left. After a year and a half, the property had gone up in value. He and his girlfriend decided to buy another place and cash in on his remaining eligibility. But they did not want to sell the house. The whole idea was to hold on to it and then get a second one so they would get appreciation on two houses instead of one. But in order to do that, they had to get around the owner-occupant, only-one-loan-at-a-time rule.

How did they do it? With a simple, outrageous, and slightly dishonest ploy. The girlfriend wrote a letter to the Veterans Administration explaining that she had bought a house with a man using his VA eligibility but had then discovered he was a homosexual. They had parted on friendly terms but obviously could no longer go on living together; she did not have any place to go so she kept the house even though she did not have the money to buy him out and take over the loan. Therefore, she would be occupying the house even though the loan itself would still be in his name and he wanted to buy a new home for himself.

Under the "special circumstances," a waiver was granted and her boyfriend, who was not a homosexual, was able to get a second loan in order to take advantage of his remaining VA eligibility. This couple got away with it, but if they had been caught it would have been a different story. What they did makes a good story, but it is highly illegal and, of course, I do not recommend it. (They could have "sold" the house to a friend or relative who would then have taken over the loan.)

Once title to the property and the loan changes ownership, the veteran is free to apply for a new VA loan up to the limits of his remaining eligibility. This would be perfectly legal. It would also be fairly easy to do, since there wouldn't have to be any down payment involved. The buyer could "buy" the property for exactly the amount of the VA loan.

Remember, VA loans are automatically assumable just like FHA loans. The new buyer doesn't have to be a veteran. Once the original owner has found a new property and gotten a new VA loan, he can even buy his house back by taking over the loan again. This is also perfectly legal. Of course, he would encounter closing costs and escrow fees each time, and it is not something you would want to try on a regular basis. But it is better than lying to the Veterans Administration and hoping you won't get caught.

Interest-Rate Ceiling on VA Loans

The interest rate lenders are allowed to charge for VA loans is fixed by the Veterans Administration in Washington. This works the same way that it works with FHA loans. Lenders make up any gap in the interest rate between conventional loans and VA loans by raising the number of points they charge to sellers. There is no indication at this time that the Veterans Administration will follow the HUD Secretary's lead and let the interest rate float with the interest rate on conventional loans. Therefore, they will probably remain more popular with buyers than they are with sellers, and veterans will continue to be turned down by sellers who refuse to pay high points.

FHA Homes for Servicemen (Section 222)

Veterans Administration loans are for veterans, so FHA has a special program for military personnel on active duty. This program allows the departments of Defense, Transportation, or Commerce to pay the HUD mortgage insurance premium for military personnel (including members of the Coast Guard) who are currently on active duty. It is also open to employees of the National Oceanic and Atmospheric Ad-

51

ministration who have been on active duty for at least two years. The program lowers the mortgage payments for these active-duty service personnel. The mortgage can be on single-family homes and condominiums only; applicants must meet all the normal requirements for an FHA loan.

ARMED SERVICES HOUSING FOR CIVILIAN EMPLOYEES (FHA SECTION 809)

If you are not in the military but work for the military as a civilian employee, FHA has a special program for you, too. If you are in an isolated location and are an employee of the National Aeronautics and Space Administration, the Nuclear Regulatory Commission, or a contractor working for either of those agencies, you might qualify. Your mortgage must qualify for HUD insurance under the basic homeowners' program, Section 203(b), and you must prove that there is too much demand for loans in your area, enough to offset any future personnel reductions at the installation where you are working. You must also be certified as eligible to participate in this program by the Secretary of Defense, the NASA Administrator, or the Nuclear Regulatory Commissioner. (When I say this is a specialized program, I mean this really is a specialized program.)

HOMEOWNERSHIP ASSISTANCE FOR LOW- AND MODERATE-INCOME FAMILIES (SECTION 221(d)(2))

If you are a low- or moderate-income prospective homebuyer, there are programs for you too, particularly if you have been displaced by urban renewal. Anyone can apply, but if your family has been displaced, you can qualify for special terms. If you haven't been displaced, the maximum loan amount is $31,000 for a single-family home ($36,000 in high-cost areas) or $36,000 and $42,000 for families of five or more. You can get larger loans for the purchase of owner-occupied buildings with two to four units.

Again, I want to stress that this isn't charity. The loans must be repaid or you will lose the property to foreclosure, and you must qualify in order to get a loan in the first place. The difference is that the qualifications are less strict than they are for regular FHA loans, since this is a special program designed to help people who would not ordinarily qualify for homeownership.

SPECIAL CREDIT RISKS (SECTION 237)

This is another special program you very well might be able to take advantage of if you ordinarily would not qualify for a home mortgage. If you are considered a marginal credit risk, you can receive counseling on budget and debt management as well as insurance for your mortgage through HUD.

The counseling services are provided through local organizations approved by HUD, while the mortgage assistance is from FHA. You merely apply for any of the usual FHA programs and ask for credit assistance. In order to get it, you must be a low- or moderate-income family with credit records indicating that you have the basic ability to handle your finances with some counseling and direction. The insured mortgage limit is $18,000 ($21,000 in high-cost areas). That may not sound like much, but if you are a low-income family with poor credit, it could be your best or even your only chance to get started with a home of your own.

An $18,000 mortgage is not going to buy you a mansion, but in many areas it will still get you a decent starter home and it will be better than renting. It will also give you a chance to get your credit on the right track.

HOUSING IN DECLINING NEIGHBORHOODS (SECTION 223(e))

If you are a homeowner or landlord or prospective homeowner in an area that has been red-lined, this program is for you. Red-lining is when lenders decide that an area has gone bad and they no longer want to make loans there. Of course, this just accelerates the process of deterioration.

If the neighborhood was bad before, it can only get worse after being red-lined. If people can't get loans to buy and then rehabilitate properties, the neighborhood has nowhere to go but downhill. In order to combat this trend, HUD has come up with a program to insure lenders against losses on mortgage loans for purchasing, rehabbing, and building housing in declining but still viable neighborhoods in urban areas.

If your area is bad enough so that the normal conditions for HUD insurance cannot be met, it is a prime candidate for this program. The program relaxes the normal requirements for HUD insurance but specifies that the property must be an "acceptable risk," a nice, ambiguous term which leaves everything wide open to interpretation.

The individual homeowners or landlords must be eligible for FHA financing under the individual programs they wish to apply for, and the terms of the loans will vary according to which program they qualify for. This is not really a separate program but an adjunct to the other HUD/FHA loan programs. It is aimed at helping affected areas rather than individuals.

Property-owners or would-be owners who do not qualify for FHA financing under one of the normal FHA loan programs will have to apply for one of the special programs aimed at helping moderate- and low-income people and those with marginal credit.

Farmers Home Administration (FmHA) Homeownership Loans

You don't even have to be a farmer to qualify for this program, just a member of a low-income family in a rural area. As a matter of fact, you do not even have to be a member of a low-income rural family to qualify. As long as you are a member of a moderate-income family in an open area (farms, scattered houses, etc.) or a town of 20,000 people or less, you could qualify for a loan from the Farmers Home Administration (FmHA).

If your family meets the above condition and is "without safe, decent and sanitary housing," and you haven't been able to get a loan from a private or commercial lender (a bank, savings and loan, or mortgage company) on reasonable terms, then rush down to your nearest FmHA office.

You will have to qualify for the loan and prove that you are capable of making the payments and keeping up with the insurance, taxes, maintenance, etc., but you can get 100% financing at reasonable interest rates. The homeownership loans can be used to buy, build, improve, repair, or rehab rural homes and related facilities, including providing adequate water and waste disposal systems, modernizing homes, adding bathrooms or central heating, or for other improvements, such as repairing driveways or foundations.

There is no set limit on the dollar amount or the interest rate for loans. These are set according to local conditions and vary from county to county. Loans of up to 100% of the cost can be granted for new construction provided the construction has been inspected by FmHA or parties approved by FmHA. The purchase of homes over one year old and improvements to those homes may also be financed with 100% loans with repayment terms up to 33 years.

FmHA loans may also be refinanced through a commercial lender at a later date, and there is no prepayment penalty. Under certain circumstances they are assumable, but a new buyer may be blocked from taking over an existing FmHA loan if FmHA objects. The FmHA county supervisor is the one who normally rules on the eligibility of applicants. Applicants or builders are expected to provide detailed building plans and cost estimates where new construction is involved.

Homes are expected to be modest in size and cost, with about 1,050 square feet of living space the average for new homes. But there are no set limits on cost, since this will vary from region to region. Homes must be located on desirable sites with an assured supply of safe drinking water and suitable arrangements for sewage disposal. Funds may be included in the loans to finance lawn seeding and landscaping to beautify the houses and make them attractive additions to their communities.

CONSTRUCTION PLANS REVIEWED

The Farmers Home Administration reviews the plans and inspects the construction as it progresses. If it is a subdivision, the houses must be sited in an attractive way to avoid straight-line monotony and to accent and preserve the natural advantages of topography, trees, and shrubbery. The streets, water, and waste disposal systems must also meet FmHA requirements.

Borrowers cannot start construction or incur any debts for materials or labor until their loan has closed escrow; each loan must be adequately secured to protect the government's interest. Any loan that is for more than $2,500 or that will not be repaid in less than ten years, must be secured by a mortgage (trust deed) against the property or other property as necessary to secure the loan.

Small home improvement loans of less than $2,500 to be repaid in less than ten years may be secured, under certain conditions, by just a promissory note. In other cases, even small loans may be secured by a mortgage (trust deed) on real estate or other suitable property, but in no case shall a loan be completely unsecured.

These are loans, not grants. They must be repaid according to the established repayment schedule. Applicants are also expected to pay for the cost of all legal services necessary to guarantee satisfactory title, for credit reports, and for other closing costs. These charges may be included in the loan amount.

Farmers Home Administration Farm Ownership Loans

You can apply directly to the Farmers Home Administration (FmHA) for an insured loan up to $200,000, or you can go to a commercial lender for an FmHA-guaranteed loan for up to $300,000. However, be forewarned: Since buying and owning a farm is not like buying and owning a house, getting a farm ownership loan is not like getting a homeownership loan either.

You not only need a good credit rating, but you have to know your stuff. Once you apply for a loan, the county or area committee of the FmHA determines whether or not you are eligible. This committee consists of three people who know local farming and credit conditions and know what it takes to succeed. Before acting on your application, the committee might ask you to meet with them or they may visit the farm you want to buy. If the committee decides that you aren't eligible or likely to succeed, either the commercial lender or the county supervisor for the FmHA will work with you to help formulate a plan to make the best use of land, labor, capital, livestock, and equipment.

TEN PERCENT INTEREST AND LESS FOR FIRST-TIME HOMEBUYERS

Even if you don't think of yourself as "special," the government may help you buy a house. You don't have to be elderly or handicapped or displaced by a new freeway to qualify. You may not even have to be in a low-income family, or live in a declining neighborhood to qualify for assistance. As long as you are a first-time homebuyer, you might qualify for low-interest, subsidized loans.

You can't own any real estate and your income must fall within the range defined as "moderate" for your area. In some places in California and other high-income areas of the country, this can be as much as $30,000 or more.

HOW THE FUNDS ARE ADMINISTERED

The funds are administered through local city and county governments. They raise the money by issuing tax-exempt bonds to investors. Since the bonds are tax-exempt, they don't have to offer as much interest as competing bonds that offer taxable interest payments. This means that the local governments can offer lower-than-normal interest rates to first-time buyers by buying down the interest rate at cooperating lenders.

In some cities or counties, there are designated target areas. Either these are the only areas where first time homebuyers can qualify for the special low-interest subsidized mortgages, or else they get an even lower interest rate if they invest in a home that is in a special target area.

In other cities or counties, there are no special target areas. The whole city or county is considered a target area and first-time homebuyers can buy homes wherever they like and still qualify for the special low-interest financing. They can buy property in the worst area of town, or the best, as long as the purchase price doesn't exceed the approved limit for the area.

For example, let's say that Fred and Frieda First-Time-Homebuyer want to buy a house. They have heard there is special low-interest mortgage money available for first-time homebuyers and they want to get some of it. Their income falls within the prescribed limits—exactly what those prescribed limits are will depend on whether they have children and what the average income is in their area—so they fill out an application. (If they are lucky, there may still be money left. If not, they are out of luck, no matter how qualified they are. Local governments cannot issue as many tax-exempt bonds as they like. In fact, there have been several attempts in Congress to restrict their use, or eliminate them entirely. Therefore, most areas have a quota that doesn't come close to meeting the demand. In an average area of a million people, a couple of thousand will be lucky enough to get one of these loans.)

WHERE CHOICE IS RESTRICTED

Then, Fred and Frieda go out looking for houses. They are given a map of the city or county, with certain areas marked in red. These are the target areas. This is where they have to buy if they want the special low-interest mortgage money. It restricts their choice of where to live, but it can also reduce their cost of living. If normal interest rates are 14% per annum, they might get a loan at 12% or even 6% for buying a home in a target area.

Or they might be able to get a loan at 12% interest no matter where they buy a house (as long as the purchase price is within the prescribed limits for the area), just because they are first-time homebuyers and their income doesn't exceed the maximum amount allowed in order to qualify for the program in their area. But, if they voluntarily buy a house in a designated target area, they may be able to get a loan at 10% interest.

Or they may find there is no designated target area, and as long as they buy a house whose purchase price doesn't exceed the maximum purchase price allowed for the area and the size of their family, they can buy a house anywhere and still qualify for 12% or even 10% interest.

Check with your local city or county government about the availability of funds in your area and requirements for qualifying (and see Chapter Eight, "Government Loan Programs for Investors," for information on tax-exempt revenue bonds for development of commercial properties and businesses).

CREDIT SERVICE AND ADVICE

Before a loan is made, it must be clear that the applicant has income to meet operating expenses as well as family living expenses, with enough left over to repay the loan and any other debts. In certain cases, the county supervisor will assist the applicant in contacting creditors to see if existing debts can be adjusted or consolidated and stretched out over a longer period of time. This credit service is designed to help those farmers who are in financial trouble and need help working out their financial affairs.

FmHA farm ownership loans are also accompanied by technical advice to help borrowers make profitable use of their farms and available resources. You will receive advice on keeping records of expenses and income, on budgeting, and otherwise making good use of your income and credit.

It doesn't cost anything to apply for an FmHA farm ownership loan, but if you apply for a guaranteed loan through a commercial lender, they may charge a reasonable loan processing fee, appraisal fee, etc., if the loan goes through. For further information, contact your local county FmHA office.

KEY POINTS TO REMEMBER

1. **Veterans Administration (VA) Loans**
   As a qualified veteran you are eligible to borrow up to $135,000 with no down payment, but you must also have the in-

come and credit to qualify for the payments. Whatever amount you do borrow is then deducted from your future eligibility until the loan is paid off or assumed by another qualified veteran.

2. Armed Services Housing for Civilian Employees (FHA Section 809)

If you are a civilian employee of the military and are located in an area with a shortage of housing and/or mortgage money caused by the presence of a military base, this special program can help you get an FHA-insured mortgage.

3. Homes for Servicemen Program (FHA Section 221)

If you are on active duty with the armed forces, this special program allows the departments of Defense, Transportation, or Commerce (depending on which government department you are under the jurisdiction of) to pay for your FHA mortgage insurance, thereby lowering your payments.

4. Homeownership Assistance for Low- and Moderate-Income Families (FHA Section 211(d)(2))

If you are a low- or moderate-income family, this FHA program can help put you in a home of your own. If you have been displaced by urban renewal, you can also qualify for special loan terms.

5. Special Credit Risks (FHA Section 237)

If you are a low- or moderate-income family or have marginal credit, but your record indicates that you should be capable of keeping up with the mortgage payments, this program can help you get a mortgage. You will also be given help with budgeting, financial planning, etc.

6. Housing in Declining Neighborhoods (FHA Section 223)

Do you live or own rental property in "Red-Line City," where the banks and mortgage companies don't want to loan any money? If so, this is the program you need. It provides insurance on mortgages in so-called marginal areas, so that lenders will be willing to issue mortgages.

7. Farmers Home Administration (FmHA) Homeownership Loans

FmHA is a division of the Department of Agriculture and makes loans to low- and moderate-income homebuyers in rural areas and towns of less than 20,000 people. They can be used for single-family or multi-family housing, new or existing, as long as they are modest in size and cost and will be owner-occupied.

8. Farmers Home Administration Farm Ownership Loans

Almost any low- or moderate-income family that can meet the payments can qualify for an FmHA Homeownership Loan. But to get a Farm Ownership Loan, you have to prove that you can make it as a farmer. You must be approved by a local committee; if you qualify, you will be given educational, technical, and financial assistance to get you started the right way.

CHAPTER FOUR

ACQUIRING PROPERTIES WITH NO CASH OR CREDIT

GOVERNMENT LOANS ARE FULLY ASSUMABLE and this is one of their greatest features. It may not seem like any big deal at first, but in times of rising interest rates or tight money, it can be extremely useful. Just think about getting 7% or 8% loans in a world where everyone else is paying 13% to 15% and you can begin to see the value and potential of government loans.

YOU MAY NOT EVEN HAVE TO QUALIFY to take over an existing loan. The original borrower may have had to go through all sorts of traumas to get the loan, producing income and expense statements, credit and employment histories, etc., but you can just march in, pay a small fee and avoid all that. For example, you don't even have to be a veteran to assume a Veterans Administration loan.

The theory behind this policy is simple. If you make loans difficult to assume then you are interfering with the property-owner's ability to sell the property. These loan programs are meant to help people, so that lets out the idea of unassumable loans. It would also not be very sound policy for the government to make it difficult to assume existing government loans. If you restrict people's ability to sell their property, you are going to have more foreclosures on your hands. People's situations change: They lose their jobs. They get divorced. Things happen which make them unable to hold on to their properties and make the payments. If they cannot make the payments and they cannot sell the property easily, then you have trouble. That is when they go into default and then, eventually, into foreclosure.

No lender wants foreclosures. From the lender's point of veiw, they are nasty, bothersome things (which we will cover in detail in another chapter). Most lenders have more than enough of them, more than they can comfortably handle.

The federal government and federally-approved lenders surely don't want any more foreclosures than they have to deal with. Foreclosures put them in the position of bad guys, taking away people's properties. Assumable loans help keep the problem down to manageable proportions. If borrowers get behind in their payments, they can always sell their properties and let someone else take over their loans. They don't have to let the properties go to foreclosure for lack of financing.

This also serves to keep building projects going when they might otherwise go under. If a developer of housing for the elderly and the handicapped, for example, defaults on his loan obligations, what is the government to do? The residents or would-be residents should not be penalized. It is not their fault, so why should they be deprived of a decent place to live?

The government can take over the projects and run them, but that is a short-term solution at best. It has been proven time and time again that the government has no business in the housing business, except as a financial backer for private organizations, profit- and nonprofit-oriented developers and managers. When it comes to owning and managing rental properties, the government is a failure. It does a terrible job.

So this is what the government usually does: It takes over bankrupt projects, but only until it can find someone suitable to take them over on a more permanent basis. The government will take bids and examine the applicants' credentials, but it is easier for everyone if the original borrower finds someone to take over the project, instead of letting the government take it over at all.

STRATEGIES FOR TURNING ASSUMABLE GOVERNMENT LOANS INTO WEALTH

Now we are going to look at some of the ways that you can use these assumable loans to put money in your pocket and equity in your retirement portfolio. It is one thing to say that assumable government loans can help make you rich because you pay 7% or 8% interest, instead of 13% to 15%. It is another matter to actually convince sellers to let you assume their low-interest assumable loans at the original interest rate. Therefore, we are going to run through some specific techniques to use in various situations.

We are going to start with the simplest transaction and work our way up from there. We are going to start off by just paying cash to the existing loan and then proceed from there. We will go through ways to assume the existing loan without putting up any cash of our own and other ways to assume the existing loans with no cash at all.

Government programs work very well with no-money-down financing techniques because the rules on assumptions are clear: Unless the lender can prove that you would harm the property and/or that you are a bad credit risk (and the burden of proof is on him, not on you), the lender has to let you assume the loan. He can charge you a small fee, but that is it. That is really the only obstacle that he can put in your way. But let's start even more simply than that, as simply as can be.

TECHNIQUE NUMBER ONE: CASH TO THE EXISTING LOAN (YOUR OWN)

Bob and Betty are back with us once again. They own some investment property now, they have some experience dealing with government loan programs, and they are in the market for properties with assumable government loans. They want deals they can close quickly. They know an assumption can close escrow within a week and that appeals to them.

(By the way, if some of you are wondering why I keep using Bob and Betty for almost all my examples, it is because they are real. Multiplied by the hundreds and thousands, they are all the people who have taken the Lowry Seminars over the years or read my books and then took exactly the path Bob and Betty Bluecollar took, exactly the path that Al and Darlene Lowry took, from their first home or small apartment building to larger and larger projects. Thousands of my students have gone on to become wealthy by investing in real estate and many of them have done it at least partially with the help of various government programs that we cover in the seminar—and that is how they have done it, one step at a time.)

They start looking through the newspaper. Pretty soon they see an ad for a house with an assumable FHA loan. It is in a good area, one they are interested in, so they decide to go and check it out, to see if it really suits them.

When they get there, they see that both the neighborhood and the house are well kept. The owners appear cheerful and friendly, relaxed and smiling. They do not seem to be at all desperate to sell and after talking to them, Bob and Betty find out that this is true. The owners want to buy another house, but they are resigned to the idea of staying in the one they have. They would like to move, but they are not unhappy where they are. They just happened to find one specific house they are interested in and if they can get the right price for their house—and the right amount of cash—they will buy it. If they can't, they will happily stay put.

Upon further discussion, it becomes clear that the real problem is not the price. It is the amount of cash they need. The house they want to buy is a bargain, so they are willing to let their house go for a reasonable price, but only if they can get enough cash out of the transaction. They are willing to deal on the price but not on the issue of the down payment. They are asking $70,000 for the house and they have a $50,000 assumable loan at 9%. They insist on cash to the loan, but so far no buyers have agreed to those terms.

The feeling that Bob and Betty get is that the sellers would actually take $65,000 or possibly even $60,000. Since Bob and Betty figure that the house is worth $70,000 to $75,000, they decide that this can be a good deal if they can get it at the right price. They have cash and they don't mind using it, because they are in a volatile business and they want the stability of knowing that there is some equity in the property and some positive cash flow coming in to support them when they get cash poor. So they make an offer of $60,000 and wind up buying the property for $62,500.

They give the sellers $12,500 in cash and they take over the existing loan. They pay the lender an assumption fee of less than $100; they sign some papers and that's it. The property and the 9% loan that goes with it are theirs. All they have to do is find a tenant and they are set.

What did they accomplish by doing this? Well, first of all, they got a $70,000 to $75,000 property for only $62,500. How? Simply because the owners wanted cash and they did not have to ask the owners to carry any paper. Cash speaks loudly when you are dealing with assumable loans.

In this case, the owners did not need to sell. Imagine if they did. If they really were desperate for cash, then Bob and Betty might have been able to give them only $5,000, or even $1,000, and then they could have just taken over the loan with almost no down payment.

The payments on their $50,000 loan are approximately $402 a month. If they had gotten a new loan for $50,000, the interest rate would be at least 13.5%, since they are investors, so the payments would be approximately $572 a month, a difference of $170 per month. Moreover, they would have had to pay a loan fee of about 3% of the loan amount, or $1,500. This is assuming that it was a conventional loan and that conventional loans for non-owner-occupants were even available in their area. In many areas, investor loans dry up as soon as money gets tight.

Even if investor loans are available in their area, Bob and Betty probably could not borrow $50,000, because that is slightly more than 80% of the purchase price and most lenders won't give investors more than 60% to 70% of the purchase price, 80% maximum. If it was an FHA investor loan, they could borrow a maximum of $50,893.75. This rather arbitrary-sounding figure is 85% of what a homebuyer would be able to borrow on a purchase price of $62,500. They would have a loan fee to pay again and the interest rate would still be about 13.5%. It would probably take at least six weeks to process the new loan instead of one week for the assumption.

A difference of $170 a month could make quite a difference to their cash flow situation. Plus, the $1,500 that they will save on loan fees is not chicken feed either. All in all, they come out way ahead and they haven't even begun to tap the potential of assumable loans.

TECHNIQUE NUMBER TWO: CASH TO THE LOAN (BORROWED)

As long as Bob and Betty had the cash anyway and wanted to keep their payments low, it made sense for them to put up a down payment.

But what if they didn't have the cash, or just didn't want to spend it? What could they do then?

They could borrow the money they need, or even better, they could have the seller borrow it for them. If the seller's house is really worth $75,000, then he ought to be able to borrow up to $60,000 or $10,000 more than the existing liens against the property. If he can borrow $10,000 of the $12,500 that they want for a down payment, then Bob and Betty will only have to come up with $2,500 on their own.

Why should the seller be willing to do this? For the obvious reason that he is still getting what he wants. He is getting his house sold, he is getting his price, and he is getting cash. Why shouldn't he be willing to do a little work?

But what if he is not willing to do this? Then Bob and Betty have to go out and get a second loan all on their own. Assuming that they have decent credit, they should be able to borrow another $10,000 to help them buy the house. If they are really short of cash, they can even try to get the seller to lower the price to $60,000 or less. If that is the only way that they can afford to buy the property and the seller really wants to sell, they will work out a deal somehow.

TECHNIQUE NUMBER THREE: ASSUMING THE LOAN WITH NO CASH DOWN

The third technique is the simplest of all, if you find the right seller. The seller that Bob and Betty were dealing with was not very motivated, so this technique just wouldn't work. But, if he really was anxious to be rid of the property, then he would deal.

What kind of seller is in that position? First of all, there is the seller who is behind in his payments or is about to fall behind. He needs to get out quickly, before he loses everything and his credit besides. It may cost Bob and Betty a little money to take over the loan, because they may have to make up a couple of back payments, but it should be well worth it.

Then there is the seller who is leaving town. He has just gotten a great job offer in another city and he needs to get going now. He doesn't have time to haggle. What he loses on the house, he will make up on his new job.

There is also the couple who are getting divorced. They can't wait to get away from each other and neither of them wants the other one to get a dime out of the house, so they will just let it go.

All of these people exist. They all exist in your area. They may not be easy to find. They may not be hanging out signs advertising the fact that they are there, but you can find them if you really look for them. And then, if you really can't find anyone who will just let you take over the property and the existing loan with no compensation, you can always try our next technique.

TECHNIQUE NUMBER FOUR: TRADE A NOTE FOR THE SELLER'S EQUITY

If the seller refuses to give up any equity that he may have in the property, then ask him to take a note for that equity instead. This way, you can still take over the existing low-interest loan and not have to come up with any cash out of your pocket. As a matter of fact, this may even be better than either Technique Number One or Technique Number Two, if you can get the seller to go along with it, except that you will not have the leverage you get when you are offering the seller all cash.

This technique is very simple. You find a seller who does not need cash, or at least does not insist on it, and start by convincing him of the tax advantages of accepting an investment sale as opposed to cashing out. Make it seem as though the installment sale will benefit him as much as you and that you are doing him a favor.

You start off asking him to carry his equity with no payments at all, for as long as possible. That is your bargaining position to start from. You can loosen up a little if necessary, but that is where you want to begin. Why? Because any time that you can get the seller's money or anyone else's at a low interest rate, with no payments, you are making money. If you don't want to invest it or use it in some other way, then you can just put it in the bank and make money on the interest rate spread.

How do you know that you are going to get a low interest rate from the seller? Because you are going to ask for it. It's as simple as that. Why shouldn't the seller give you a low interest rate? After all, he's not a banker or a mortgage broker. He's not in the business of loaning money and getting paid for it. He is just trying to get his property sold.

You don't necessarily want to ask for the same interest rate that the first loan carries, unless you know the seller is really motivated, for one reason or another. Many buyers try to use the argument that since the interest rate on the first loan is just right, then the interest rate on the second loan should also be reasonable, but sellers usually respond that since the first loan is so inexpensive, the buyer is getting a real bargain and should pay more for the property. Generally, it is better to offer more interest than he would get by keeping his money in the bank but less than you would have to pay to get a second loan from someone else. Since he could get as little as 5.5% by putting his money in the bank, this gives you a lot of room to maneuver.

Sometimes, you can play with the interest rate, the price, and the terms until you find out what the seller's real weak spot is. What is it that he really wants most? Does he want his asking price? Does he want a short payback period? Does he want a higher interest rate? He can't have it all, so what does he want? What can you most easily afford to give up, since you probably can't get everything that you want, either?

If the seller won't accept a note with no payments, then offer to make payments each month. If he balks at the length of the loan term and wants to get paid off faster, then see if you can negotiate a shorter loan term. And if none of that works (because the seller is concerned about his security and doesn't want to carry a second loan), there is another approach you can use.

TECHNIQUE NUMBER FIVE: THE WRAPAROUND

If a seller does not feel that carrying a second mortgage will give him enough security for his equity, then let him carry a first mortgage instead. That way, he will not have to worry about losing out in case of a foreclosure. There will not be anyone in front of him, standing in line, waiting to collect money before he does.

That should go a long way toward making the seller feel better, but how can you do it? After all, there already is a first mortgage against the property. If you add another mortgage, one of them has to go into second position.

This is where the wraparound, also known as the all-inclusive, or over-riding deed of trust or mortgage, comes in. The seller keeps making the payments on his original mortgage and then he carries a new, larger first mortgage for you. The difference between what you pay him and what he pays on the original first mortgage goes into his pocket.

Let's say, for example, that Bob and Betty did not want to put down any money when they bought that house for $62,500 and assumed a first mortgage of $50,000. If the seller carried a wraparound mortgage for the whole purchase price, they would make payments to him, based on a loan of $62,500. He would make payments to the original lender, based on a loan of $50,000. Assuming that the interest on the wraparound loan would be 9%—the same as the interest rate on the original $50,000 loan—the seller would put approximately $100 in his pocket each month. Plus, he will have the security of being in first position. If the buyer stops making payments he will know right away and he can foreclose immediately.

When absolutely necessary, you can even offer the seller a higher interest rate on the wraparound loan that he will carry. Or you can assume a low interest rate loan, create your own wraparound loan, and then offer the property to a new buyer at a slightly higher price and interest rate. This can be an excellent way to make money.

For example, let's say that Bob and Betty get that house for $62,500 with the seller carrying the entire loan at 9% interest. The property is worth as much as $75,000 and interest rates are at least 13%, even for owner-occupants, so $70,000 with $5,000 down and a $65,000 loan at 11% is still a good deal for someone. The new buyer gets a decent price and a good interest rate. Bob and Betty get $5,000 cash and a small monthly income. This is a perfect example of a win-win transaction where everyone comes out ahead.

Technique Number Six: Borrowed Cash and a Note as Down Payment

There are going to be times when even the wraparound won't work. There are some sellers who insist on cash. It's not security that they are concerned with, it's cold, hard, spending money that they can hold in their hands. But that doesn't mean that they need to have all cash.

Be creative. Explore the possibilities. If the seller insists that he needs cash, find out just how much (or rather, just how little) he really needs and then see if he will carry the balance of the equity. For example, Bob and Betty might have put down $5,000 and then asked the seller to carry the remaining $7,500 of the purchase price. If they didn't have $7,500 of their own money to put down or just didn't want to use their own money, they could have gotten a $5,000 second mortgage, or had the seller get it, and then they could have asked the seller to carry the remaining $7,500 as a third mortgage. As long as they are getting their cash, many sellers will go along with this in spite of being in third position.

KEY POINTS TO REMEMBER

1. Most government loans are automatically assumable.
2. You don't have to qualify to assume government loans.
3. You can assume government loans at the original interest rates.
4. You can assume an existing loan, wrap it, and then resell the property at a higher price and interest rate.
5. By offering cash to the loan, you may get a lower price.

CHAPTER FIVE

GETTING CASH BACK AT THE CLOSING

OVERFINANCING

Getting cash back at the close of escrow is easy with assumable loans. All you have to do is convince the seller to finance the property for more than the purchase price. This can be done legally or it can be done illegally, ethically or unethically. Mostly, it depends on who gets the second loan—the buyer or the seller—and how much they understand about what they are really committing themselves to.

THE SELLER GETS THE SECOND LOAN. Then it is none of the lender's business whether or not you overfinance the property. The second loan is being made on the basis of the property's value, not the purchase price. If you get the second loan as a purchase money loan, then you have to read the fine print. Some loans forbid you to take on any additional loans without the lender's permission. If that is the case, then you can, theoretically, be in trouble, if the lender finds out.

The lender may never find out and then again, the lender might. If anything ever goes wrong, then everything could really compound. Then the lender could call the second loan due and insist on immediate payment. The lender could even press charges for fraud (although this isn't very likely, unless you do this with a whole string of properties). The seller could possibly sue you for damages. It's a dangerous game to play.

What is even more dangerous and definitely illegal is to lie about the purchase price. Some buyers and sellers deliberately conspire to defraud the lender. They pump up the purchase price and get the lender to make a bigger loan that way. This works when the lender makes loans based on the purchase price, not the appraised value. It works, but it can get you into a lot of trouble. The safe way to get cash back at the close of escrow is to have the seller get the second loan for more money than he needs for the down payment.

For example, let's say that Bob and Betty find a good property to buy. It is worth about $80,000 and the seller is asking $70,000, with cash down to the $50,000 assumable loan. After a lot of wrangling back and forth, the seller agrees on a purchase price of $62,500, with a $5,000 cash down payment.

However, Bob and Betty don't want to take $5,000 in cash out of their pocket. They want to get into the property with no money down. In fact, they want to put money in their pocket. They want to be paid for buying the property. How can they satisfy the seller's needs and their own, all at the same time?

The answer lies in the property. There is enough equity there to finance the sale and more. The seller goes out and borrows $10,000 on a second mortgage and gives half of that to Bob and Betty at the close of escrow. Bob and Betty take over the payments on the $10,000 second mortgage. Then they give the seller a note for $7,500, backed by a third mortgage (trust deed) against the property, for the balance of the purchase price.

Remember, the key to all this is that there is plenty of equity in the property. The lender is making the $10,000 second loan on the basis of the property's supposed value of $80,000, which gives the seller $30,000 in equity. Since the lender will loan up to a total of 80% of the value, or $64,000, the seller could borrow up to $14,000 if he wanted to. This is why he should have no trouble getting a $10,000 loan, because that is still well within the equity cushion the lender requires.

The lender doesn't have to know that the property is going to be sold. In fact, it's none of the lender's business what the seller intends to do with the property. The lender is making the loan based on the equity in the property and the seller's credit, not the fact that someone else wants to purchase the property for any given amount. As long as the second loan is assumable, then it is up to the buyer and seller to work out their own arrangements without any interference from the lender; since FHA and VA first loans are always automatically assumable, there won't be any trouble there. That's what makes government loans so easy and so profitable to work with.

You don't even have to give the seller any of the money. Theoretically, you could agree to buy the property for $50,000, exactly the amount of the existing loan, then have the seller go and pull some cash out of the property and give it all to you. As long as the seller understands what he's doing and goes along with you, you're okay.

IF YOU CAN'T GET THE SELLER TO GET THE SECOND LOAN, then just be very, very careful about reading the fine print in the second loan agreement. Is the lender basing the loan amount upon the purchase price or upon the value of the property as established by an appraiser? If an appraiser has established the value of the property, then the purchase price really shouldn't matter. But if the loan amount is supposed to be based on the purchase price, then the only way you are going to get the loan amount you need is to lie, and that is no solution at all.

If the lender knows what you are really paying for the property and understands how you are trying to finance it, you will never get any money. You will be turned down flat. Why? Because the lender will feel that there is inadequate security for the loan. Since you won't have anything invested in the property, there won't be anything to stop you from walking away if anything goes wrong. You won't have any real commitment to the property.

Lenders don't like that. They want you to be committed to holding on to the property through thick and thin. They want to know that you will suffer a definite financial loss if you do walk away from the property, so that you won't just leave them stuck. This is why they usually are easier to deal with if they think that you already own the property. Then they don't worry about how much cash you have invested in the property, only about how much the property is worth.

GET THE SELLER TO SIGN THE PROPERTY OVER TO YOU now and agree to wait at least 45 to 60 days for any down payment money he is supposed to get and before recording any notes he will carry. This way, when you go to a lender, all he will have to know is that you own the property and that it is either free and clear or has one loan against it. He doesn't have to know what you paid for it, or how many loans you are going to add later, or any of that. It's all irrelevant.

Let's say, for example, that the seller refused to get the second loan for Bob and Betty. Either he just doesn't want to do it, or his credit is bad, or there is some other reason why he can't get the loan, but that idea just won't work, for whatever reason. Bob and Betty could just give up, or go and find another property, but they don't. Instead, they come up with a creative alternative. They get the seller to sign the property over to them immediately. In exchange, they give him two notes, one for $5,000 and one for $7,500. The $5,000 note is all due and payable within 60 days. It is a personal note, unsecured, with no interest. The $7,500 note is due and payable in five years with interest of 12% per annum. It is to be secured by a mortgage (deed of trust) against the property, but there is a clause in there stating that it will not be recorded for at least 60 days after the close of escrow and that it will automatically subordinate, or become a secondary lien, to any new financing the buyer may decide to add to the existing $50,000 loan.

This allows Bob and Betty to take over the property and assume the first loan. They go to a lender and get a $10,000 second loan, based on the $30,000 equity they have in the property. They give the seller $5,000 to pay off the first note and pocket the other $5,000. The seller records the other note for $7,500 and that goes into third position, behind the $50,000 first and the $10,000 second. Bob and Betty still have about $12,500 in equity and everyone's happy.

Another safe way to do it is to write in the contract that the seller is to leave you money for repairs in escrow. That way, it is right out in the open that you are getting cash back and the lender or the seller cannot claim that you tried to defraud anyone. Lenders will often go along with this because they feel that by improving the property you are increasing the security for the loan. Some of them will require contractors' estimates or that the money be held in escrow until the repairs are completed, but most lenders will not really worry about what you intend to do with the money once you get it, as long as it all looks good on paper. They want to be protected by having it in their records that you used the money for repairs, but in real life, they don't care.

You Can Also Get Cash Back at Closing by Using Discounted Notes. If you can get the seller to accept a note secured by another piece of property, instead of the one that you are buying, you can put cash in your pocket and accumulate equity besides.

What you do is go out and buy a discounted note. If the seller agrees to take a note for $12,500 at 11% interest, then you go out and buy a note like that for anywhere from $6,000 to $9,000 and pocket the difference. This is done every day and it is perfectly safe and legal as long as you don't conceal anything from the seller or the lender.

For example, let's say Bob and Betty use a technique known as the substitution-of-collateral clause. They start off by giving the seller his full asking price of $90,000, just to put him in a good mood. They take over an existing loan of $50,000 and agree to give the seller $5,000 in cash and a note at 15% interest, all due in seven years, for the $35,000 balance. Now, here's where the creative part comes in. They put a clause into the purchase contract that states that they have the right to substitute alternative collateral of equal or greater value for the note the seller agreed to carry. On the open market, a straight note with a seven-year due date and 15% interest is worth somewhere between 40% and 60% of the face value, if it's a second note. Third notes are worth about 30% of face value, so Bob and Betty go out looking for a note to buy. They find a $35,000 note at 15% interest that they can buy for $10,000. The only trouble is that they don't have $10,000 in cash. They want to finance the purchase of the note with no money down and cash in their pocket at the close of escrow.

It is time for some more creative thinking. They don't have $10,000 in cash and they wouldn't want to spend it if they did. They do have $100 though, and they give that to the noteholder in exchange for an option to buy the note within 60 days. If they buy the note, the $100 counts toward the $10,000 purchase price. If they don't buy the note within that time period, they forfeit the $100.

Bob and Betty get the seller to agree to subordinate his $35,000 note to any additional financing that they may add in the future and to wait 60 days after the close of escrow before recording it. Then they go to a lender, tell him that they own a property that is worth approximately $100,000 and has a $50,000 first loan against it, and that they would like to get a second loan for $30,000.

This loan takes about 45 days to go through; they then take the money and give $5,000 to the person they're buying the property from. They give $9,900 to the holder of the $35,000 note they have optioned and pocket the rest. They have paid off both notes 15 days ahead of schedule and they have picked up $20,000 worth of equity, in addition to the cash.

How?

They go to the seller of the property and offer him their $35,000 note

81

for his. The interest rate is the same, but their note is more attractive because it has a five-year due date. That leaves them with only two liens against the property, a $50,000 first and a $30,000 second.

BECOMING A GOVERNMENT-APPROVED CONTRACTOR is another good way to get cash back when you close escrow. Think about many of the things that you have heard about contractors who work with the government. Many of them are true. The government can be a very generous employer or partner and you don't have to cheat and do anything dishonest to profit handsomely from this generosity. Just by playing within the rules you should be able to make a lot of money.

What do you have to do to become a government-approved contractor? That depends on where you live. What are the requirements for a contractor's license in your state? Sometimes you just pay a small fee and you don't even have to pass any tests or anything. The first thing you have to do is to find out what the rules are where you plan to do business.

Most states will let property-owners work on their own properties without any sort of license at all and the federal government will usually go along with this and allow people to act as owner-contractors. This means that you can pay yourself to work on your own project and include that in the project expenses. The government is going to loan the project money to cover the cost of your contracting services, including a profit over and above your costs as a contractor.

You mean you can actually make a profit working for yourself and then get the government to loan you the money—at least guarantee the loan—to pay yourself?

Yes. Why shouldn't you make a profit? If you hired someone else to be the contractor, then that person would make a profit, so why shouldn't you? It is just like doing the management. If you are going to do it then you should get paid for it. Besides, you are not going to be working for yourself, you are going to be working for the limited partnership. This means that your contractor's fees—including your profit as a contractor—are paid to you as soon as the project is finished. You do not have to wait five or more years until the project is sold to see your money. It all comes out of project expenses, right off the top, before anyone gets any profits from the sale or refinancing of the property and even before the limited partners get their original investment back.

You can lease equipment to the limited partnership. You can make money on the spread between what you charge for contracting services and what you pay your subcontractors. You can even get a markup on materials. It is all legal, as long as it is all open and above board and done according to the government's guidelines.

Everyone—the investors and the government—must be fully informed about what you are doing and what fees you are charging for services performed. The government sets definite limits on how much profit you can make, how high your overhead can be, and how much you can charge for any equipment that you rent to the project, but the nice part about dealing with the government as a contractor is that you can't go wrong. The government guarantees your profit.

You are allowed a certain percentage of the project's cost—usually a generous percentage, 20% or more—for your profit and overhead. Unless you are completely off on all your estimates for materials and labor, you have to come out ahead. This is the government's famous cost-plus system for dealing with bids from contractors. It is designed to make sure that no one ever loses any money by dealing with the government.

If you are a woman or a member of a minority—or in partnership with one, not just a limited partnership unless you are joint general partners, but a simple partnership—then you are even better off. Under federal law, women and minorities are to be given preferential treatment in gaining government contracts and access to grants and low-interest loans. This means that companies headed by women and minorities can get money more easily and, in some cases, more cheaply than other companies or individuals. This means that they can submit lower bids on federally sponsored jobs and still make the same profit. This can be a tremendous advantage. If nothing else, you can always guarantee yourself employment this way and make a good salary too.

Let's run through a typical situation with Bob and Betty again and see how they make out this time. They have successfully done at least one project with government funding, so now they want to try another one and this time they want to act as their own contractors. Naturally, as soon as they find out about the affirmative action rule, they form a new company, Cash Poor Construction Inc., with Betty as the president. Now they have four different companies: Elderly and Handicapped Housing Development Company is a limited partnership that develops housing for the elderly and the handicapped. The general partner is Cash Poor Investments Inc. Cash Poor Investments contracts with Cash Poor Management Inc. to manage the property once the construction/rehabilitation phase has been completed and with Cash Poor Construction Inc. to manage the actual construction and rehabilitation. Bob and Betty are employees and stockholders of all the Cash Poor companies.

The three companies do not necessarily have to be separate. The general partner could handle all three functions (general partner, general contractor, and management company). But remember, the arrangement must be clear. Any attempt to mislead either the investors or the government could get you in a lot of trouble. Assuming it is done legally, however, just look at all the sources of income Bob and Betty can develop:

First of all, they can charge a fee as general partners who put the whole deal together, and help the limited partners to get tax benefits. That is Income Source Number One.

They can charge a fee as the general contractors, managing the property during the construction/rehabilitation. This doesn't mean that they have to do any actual work on the project. Absolutely not. The work can all be hired out to subcontractors. All Bob and Betty have to do is act as overseers. That is Income Source Number Two.

Then, Bob and Betty can rent equipment to the project and make a profit on that. That is Income Source Number Three.

When the construction and rehabilitation work is done, they get a fee for managing the property for the next five years. That is Income Source Number Four.

Oh yes. There is also one more possible source of income that I forgot to mention: As general partner, Cash Poor Investments, Inc. would probably get a share in any positive cash flow that the property produced. That is Income Source Number Five.

Five sources of income from one project, one limited partnership—and two of them would not be possible if Bob and Betty did not act as their own contractor. Don't you think that you should find out what it takes to become a contractor? Couldn't you use two additional sources of income?

Non-Owner-Contractors

What about becoming a contractor for a project that you are not directly involved with? There are several government programs that do not permit profit-oriented investors to own or control the projects but do allow profit-motivated contractors to build them and then sell them or turn them over to nonprofit organizations to run.

This can be an excellent source of income if you are a legitimate licensed contractor. These projects are virtually guaranteed by the government, so you can't help but make money. Of course, you won't make nearly as much as you would by being an owner of the project. You won't get any of the appreciation or tax benefits, but this can be the next best thing. Always remember: As long as you know how to play by the rules, the government can be a very generous client to do business with.

KEY POINTS TO REMEMBER

1. If the seller gets the second loan, the purchase price is irrelevant.
2. The seller must understand that you will be overfinancing the property and what this means.
3. If the seller won't get the second loan, find a lender who bases loans on the appraised value, not the purchase price.
4. You can have the seller sign over the property and agree to subordinate his equity to any new financing.
5. With the substitution-of-collateral clause, you can use discounted notes to pick up free equity as well as instant cash.
6. Owner-contractors generally don't need any license at all.
7. The government allows owner-contractors to make a profit.
8. The government lets contractors rent themselves equipment.
9. By law, women and minority contractors get preference.
10. Profit-oriented contractors can build certain projects and then sell them to nonprofit organizations to run.

CHAPTER SIX

OPTIONS: REWARDS WITHOUT RISKS

OPTIONS AND GOVERNMENT PROGRAMS

What are options and how can they make you wealthy? Options are
choices or alternatives, the chance to do things more than one way.
The more choices we have in life the more freedom we have to operate,
to explore all the possibilities and find the best solutions to any problems we encounter.

One of the things that has always made the United States such a
great place in which to live and work, one of the main things that has
attracted so many immigrants over the centuries, has been the variety
of choices available to people in this country. Rather than being locked
in by rigid expectations or limited resources, people in this country

have always enjoyed the freedom to explore new possibilities and try many different occupations or places to live before settling down.

Having options leads to innovation and creativity. The lack of options stifles initiative. If your fate is already sealed, then why bother trying to change it and make things any better? You live with what you've got and make the best of it.

Real estate is not that different from life. The more choices you have, the more creative you can be. If you are in a strong position as a buyer and have many potential deals to choose from, you can start to play games, take chances, and see how far you can go. Will the seller carry paper? Will he carry a straight note, without any payments until the end of the loan term? Will he let you pull some cash out of the deal at the close of escrow?

The only way to find out is to ask, and the only way to find out your true limit is to go until you are stopped. When the seller finally says no and really sticks to it, then you know you have pushed as hard as you can. Or have you? One idea that many buyers don't even bother to pursue is to option properties instead of buying them outright.

OPTIONING VERSUS BUYING

By optioning the property, you are keeping yourself free and uncommitted. The owner is pledged to sell you the property but you are not pledged to buy it. It is like buying a piece of furniture or an appliance on the layaway plan. You put down a deposit and the owner agrees to hold it for you. If you eventually come up with the money to buy the item, your deposit is credited toward the purchase price.

If you decide not to buy it, the worst thing that can happen is that you lose your deposit. The store cannot force you to buy the item and can't take any other action against you for not buying it. If you bought the item with a small down payment and then decided you didn't want it, you might have a much harder time. Depending on the contract you signed, you might be liable for all the payments agreed to, even if you change your mind and decide you don't want the merchandise. If you stop making payments, the store could take the merchandise and sue you for the remaining payments at the same time.

If you are buying real estate and the seller is carrying the loan, it is easy to return the property. If you decide that you don't like the property, just stop making payments. The seller will foreclose on the mortgage or trust deed he holds against the property as security for his loan and take the property back. Of course, this won't do wonders for your credit rating.

Lenders are not enthusiastic when they see a foreclosure on your record. Therefore, you would try to get the seller to take a deed in lieu of foreclosure. This means you just sign the property back to him and he doesn't have to foreclose. Nothing goes on your credit rating, but you still lose your original down payment (if you put up anything) and any equity you have built up in the property (the difference between what you owe and what the property is worth).

Not every seller will cooperate with this, either. Many times the seller will be angry. He doesn't want the property back—especially if he sold it to you with little or nothing down. He sold it to you because he wanted to be rid of it once and for all. If you are dealing with a commercial lender, and the seller did not carry back any paper, you could really have a problem.

How are you going to get the seller to take the property back? He has his cash and your name on a contract saying you agreed to pay him a certain amount of dollars for the property. Why should he want to take the property back and return the cash, unless the property has gone up in value? The lender is not very likely to be too sympathetic, either.

If you bought the property, you are expected to make your payments, period. The lender does not care whether or not you are happy with the property, and the lender is not going to want to take the property off your hands unless there is some equity to be gained. Commercial lenders (banks, savings and loans, and mortgage companies) will foreclose if necessary, but they are not necessarily going to make any deals to save your credit rating.

DEFICIENCY JUDGMENTS

Then, of course, there is the problem of deficiency judgments. What happens if the seller or the commercial lender forecloses and the property goes up for auction and they don't even get back the amount of the loan? If the property was your own home, you don't have to worry, because the lender cannot get a deficiency judgment against you—in some states.

In other states—or if it was just a piece of income property (this would apply in just about every state)—you could be facing a deficiency judgment. The seller or commercial lender could sue you for the difference between what they got at the foreclosure auction and what you owe, including late fees, foreclosure fees, attorney fees, and court costs.

If yours is a trust deed state, where most real estate loans are secured by deeds of trust rather than mortgages, you are lucky. Most of the time, lenders do not bother going after deficiency judgments in trust deed states. If a lender chooses to foreclose under a trust deed, in those states where trust deeds are legal, there are no deficiency judgments. The lender takes what he gets at the foreclosure auction and that's it.

If the lender thinks he might want to file a deficiency judgment, he has to foreclose under a mortgage instead. If a lender wants to foreclose under a trust deed, he has his trustee file all the appropriate papers, including the notice of default and the notice of sale; then he waits at least 21 days and goes to the foreclosure sale that his trustee has set up. There are no courts involved, no lawyers, no judges. It is a nice, clean procedure and the whole thing takes about four months.

If the lender chooses to foreclose under a mortgage, he must petition a judge for permission to foreclose. He cannot just go ahead and start the proceedings because the borrower has not been making payments. It is not that simple. A mortgage foreclosure can take a year or more to wind its way through the courts, and then the borrower gets a right of redemption that he doesn't get with a trust deed foreclosure.

If the lender forecloses under a mortgage, the buyer has the right to buy the property back for up to two years in some states. If the lender forecloses under a deed of trust, the borrower has no right or redemption. Either he buys the property back before the foreclosure auction or it is gone, along with his credit rating.

Options Mean Never Having to Say You're Sorry

Options solve all these problems. If you walk away from a property you have optioned, nothing happens to your credit rating. The seller can't sue you. He can't even call you a lot of bad names, except under his breath, because you never said you would buy the property. All you ever said was that you were interested in it and you might want to buy it. *Might* . . . That is the operative word, with no promises stated or implied. Just think of all the situations where this could come in handy. Think of all the situations where it could be vital.

How can you buy properties with government assistance and commit yourself to the property before you even know if you will get the money? That is dangerous business. When you are dealing with the bureaucracy, you must assume that whatever can go wrong will go wrong, sooner or later. Problems will change or be eliminated, funds will dry up, quotas will be filled, and, when all else fails, they will lose your application.

Everything takes four times as long as you expect and at least twice as long as it should. If you are sitting there with an impatient seller on your back, waiting to get his money, it can get awfully uncomfortable. Optioning the property takes all the heat off. The seller knows you have a certain amount of time to make up your mind or come up with any money that you agreed to put down, so he can't rush you. If something goes wrong with your financing, you just don't exercise the option and that's the end of it. There are no repercussions. If the property makes sense anyway, even if you have to go for conventional financing through a commercial lender, that is another story. If you know that you want the property no matter what happens, maybe you should just buy it outright, especially if you think you can get better terms that way.

But, if the property makes sense only if the government comes in as a partner, you had better tie the property up with an option until you get your partner's approval. If the idea of an option seems one-sided, with everything weighted in your favor against the seller, that is because it *is* one-sided. It is weighted in favor of the buyer, or the possible buyer.

The seller is giving up something and the buyer isn't. It is a very simple one-sided agreement. Why would any seller want to sign an agreement like that, which gives the buyer all the privileges, while he has all the responsibilities? A seller is just a person like anyone else, so the answer is obvious—because he believes that there is something in it for him too.

Legally, there has to be something in it for the seller, otherwise there is no binding agreement. The buyer must give the seller something of value, whether it is money, or services, or some other valuable consideration, in exchange for the option.

THE "NO ALTERNATIVES" OPTION

The law says you must offer valuable consideration for an option, but the law does not say how valuable the consideration must be. That is left up to the law of the marketplace to decide. It can be as little as one dollar, if the property-owner is willing to part with an option that cheaply.

In many cases, the option fee is not the reason property-owners accept options on their properties, anyway. The real reason is that they have no alternatives. No one has made any realistic offers to buy their properties, so an option contract seems better than nothing. An option gives you control of the property, which is what you want, and it gives the seller hope, which is what he wants. If he can't get you hooked legally, at least he can try to get you hooked emotionally.

Once you are involved with the property, there is at least a chance you might buy it and if you decide not to, at least he can talk to you, try to change your mind. If no one else has made any reasonable offers, the seller may be frustrated and insecure, wondering what is wrong with his property (or even better, knowing what is wrong with it) and wishing that he had at least a potentially interested buyer to deal with.

Use this to your advantage by reminding the seller that you don't want to commit yourself to the property because you only want it if certain conditions work out, because otherwise you will never be able to get a loan—and neither will anyone else. If this is true, the property won't be worth much and there won't be a very wide market for it, especially since so few people know about the government programs that are available. You shouldn't have to pay much for the property at all, or for the option.

Without financing, who can buy the property? This is a perfect approach to use with properties in red-lined areas, or with properties that are so run down they don't qualify for normal financing. In some cases, you will be able to show the sellers how optioning their property to you is literally their only way to get it sold.

You may need to have work done on it before it can qualify for any financing at all. This means that you must have an option just to protect yourself. How can you do work on the property unless you have a recorded interest in it? That would be just throwing away your time and money. Even a seller can see that. If he wants to have the property sold, he has to cooperate with you. He gets no guarantees that way, but at least there is a chance he will sell the property.

SHORT-TERM "CONTINGENCY" OPTIONS

If you can't get the seller to agree to an option because it is the only way he will get the property sold, try making him an offer to buy the property outright. Why are we talking about buying property outright when the whole purpose of this section is to teach you how to use options so that you can avoid committing yourself to any property for as long as possible? Because making an offer and purchasing the property are two different things. If your offer is structured properly, with all the proper contingencies, you are not really committed to the property at all.

What you are really doing is asking the seller for a free short-term option, one that you won't have to pay for, simply because you don't call it an option. If your offer has contingencies in it, you are not committed to buying the property until those contingencies have been removed. If the seller accepts this, he has committed himself without requiring a real commitment from you. Call it what you will.

In effect, he has given you an option on the property until the time limit runs out for removing the contingencies. That is when you must either commit yourself or give up the property.

IF YOU CANCEL

Until then, you are in control. The seller can't deal with anyone else. He can't raise the price or change the terms. He can't sell the property or borrow any money against it without your permission. You have a signed purchase agreement.

But if you cancel the deal because one or more of the contingencies has not been met, there is nothing the seller can do. You even get your deposit back. This could give you the time to find out what you need to know. For example, if you make the offer contingent upon getting "suitable financing," it is up to you to determine what "suitable" means, since you are the one who will have to live with it. If you don't get the government loans or subsidies you want, you don't have to go through with your offer.

Of course, you can also be more direct about it and just make your offer contingent upon getting the specific loans or subsidies that you are counting on to make the project profitable. The problem with this is that it locks you in.

If your financing comes through but you decide to back out for some other reason, you will be stuck and the seller will have the right to keep your deposit. More important is that by telling the seller your plans, you may be putting ideas into his head. Once he knows what you are going to do, how you plan to get financing, he may decide he doesn't need you after all. He can either do it himself or tell other prospective buyers how to do it and see if someone else will give him a higher price. You will have shown him that there is not only potential value in the property but a way to tap that potential.

The less the seller knows about your business and what you intend to do with the property, the better. If he is going to carry the loan, that would be one thing, but if he is going to cash out anyway as soon as the contingencies are removed, then it's none of his business. Of course, he

95

may not see it that way. If you are going to be tying up his property for any length of time and taking it off the market, a smart seller is going to want more details.

The Waiting Game

How do you satisfy him without giving away too much? You start off by putting in a definite time limit. You will either get your financing or release the seller from the contract within a certain time period, say 90 days. This way, the seller knows you have a legitimate purpose in mind and do not intend to keep his property tied up indefinitely. It gives him a definite date to focus on and makes his hope to sell the property a little more real. It makes your plans to buy the property (maybe) seem more definite.

How long you can make the seller wait is an individual matter. You will just have to see how anxious each seller is and how likely he is to get a better offer from someone else. Then you will know just how far you can push. The more time you can get, the better. For one thing, it gives you more time to make your arrangements without rushing. It also gives you more time to be sure that you made the right choice.

Just because a piece of property is a good deal, it doesn't mean there are not other properties out there that are even better deals. This may not happen to you very often, but again, it doesn't have to. Every once in a while you will run across a deal that is better than some deal you are already involved with; that is when the information in this section will pay off for you.

It is always easy to "not" get a loan. All you have to do is withhold information needed to verify your income. They will turn you down every time. Once you are turned down for the loan, you are out of the deal. That is what the contract says, and besides, how could you buy the property without financing, even if you wanted to? The seller can't blame you in this situation. It's not your fault, and you are at least as disappointed as he is, so how can he be mad at you? Of course, you get your deposit back. . . .

The "Let-the-Property-Sit-There" Option

There are other times when the best way to handle the situation is to do nothing, and the best type of option to negotiate is none at all. If the property is a real borderline situation, where you might be able to make some money but you are not sure, you may not want to bother putting in an offer at all, not to option the property and not to buy it, either.

Putting in offers takes time. You have to sit down, think about what you want to say, and then get it down on paper. Then you have to meet with the seller or his agent to present the offer and spend time discussing it. You could be using all that time to be out looking at other properties, instead.

Second, making any kind of offer gives the seller hope (remember?). Why should you want to give him hope if the property is a borderline deal? In a situation like this, if you don't really think anyone else is going to come along and steal the property away from you and you don't care even if they do, you should just walk away. It's a good way to test your own feelings, if nothing else.

Once you get a little distance from the situation, you may decide that the property is more attractive than you had originally given it credit for. Or you may decide that it is even less attractive and you will forget about it entirely. You may find a better deal, or several of them, as soon as you start seriously looking. And if you don't, you can probably come back after a while and find the property still waiting for you, if you judged the situation correctly.

STRENGTHENING YOUR POSITION

The longer a property sits on the market, the less it is worth. It becomes stale, like old bread. No one wants it, because they all assume there is something wrong with it. If there isn't, why hasn't it sold? This is why you do not want to give the seller any hope in such a situation.

Let him sit there wondering why no one wants his property. Go out and do all your checking. Find out what government programs are in effect in your area and what sorts of projects are open to bidding. Explore all the possibilities you can. Make sure you investigate the full potential of the property to see if there are any ways it can be made profitable.

If you come up with the right answers, you can make your offer from a position of strength. You should know how high you are prepared to go and how much you can afford to offer, if necessary. You will start off by offering as little as you think you can get away with, but if the seller turns you down, you want to know how much you can afford to pay for the property and still make a profit. The problem here is that the applications are limited. You can make a profit this way only when the conditions are right. If anyone else is interested in the property, it won't work. While you are doing your research, they will buy the property and you will just be wasting your time.

THE FIRST-RIGHT-OF-REFUSAL OPTION

There are also certain types of information that you can't get or don't want to get until you have the property tied up with either an option or a purchase contract. If you have to put up money for application fees or other costs, you are not going to want to do so without some sort of protection. Otherwise, you are just throwing money away. Accordingly, you might tell the owner that you are interested in the property only under certain conditions and only if you can tie it up while you check to see if those conditions can be met.

If he won't accept a purchase contract with the right contingencies in it, you might just offer him a little money (or other goods or services as valuable consideration) for a first-right-of-refusal option. This would guarantee that he would not sell the property to anyone else for a specified period of time. There would be no guarantee that you would buy the property and no price set.

If you decide to buy the property, the price and terms would be set at that time. This would protect you and your rights in the property without tying you down. If you find out that the property is worth buying, you sit down with the seller and start negotiating. He is already committed to selling to you, so all you have to do is work out the details.

PROTECTING YOUR INTEREST

You want to leave the price open, because you may not know how much the place is really worth to you until you have finished all your research and found out just what funding is available. Once again, the longer you can tie up the property, the better. It gives you more time to explore alternatives and it gives the seller more time to get nervous. So try to option the property for as long as you can.

Also, try to get the seller to give up the right to consider other offers during the option period. If he can consider other offers and let other people look at the property, you could be in trouble. That is good for the seller and it is good for any competition you may have, but there is no way it can be good for you. If other people are free to look at the property and make offers, you will have to match any offers that come in. This is bound to drive up the price.

Even if no one else bids on the property, it gives the seller the idea that he is in control of the situation, not you. What you want is an option which says that the seller cannot even show the property to anyone during the option period. Until the option period runs out, or you decline to buy the property, formally, in writing, you are the only one who can inspect the property or make any offers. Then, you take this option down to your county recorder's office and have it recorded and put in the county records as a lien against the property.

Your interest is now protected. You can go out and do your research, file your applications, and get everything in motion to get your funding. Once you know that you've got it, you can sit down and work out your final deal with the seller.

THE FIXED-PRICE OPTION

There are times, though, when you will want even more security than you can get from a first-right-of-refusal option. If you are in an inflationary market, or on the verge of one, you may want to set the price and terms in advance, so you don't wind up paying more later.

If the inflation has not hit yet, it might not be too difficult to get the seller to go along with this. He might be just as happy getting everything set in advance and being that much closer to actually having the property sold. On the other hand, if prices are already on the rise, he will probably want to be paid more for a fixed-price option, because he will feel as though he is giving up more that way. You have to be prepared for this and balance it against the benefits.

Is there really going to be enough inflation to justify paying more for a fixed-price option? If the answer is yes, pay the price. If it is no, then go for the first-right-of-refusal option and take your chances.

THE ROLLING OPTION

If you really want to protect yourself against inflation and rising property values, this is the way to do it. The rolling option has rather limited applications, but when it works it can be quite a useful wealth-building tool. It allows you to use maximum leverage when you are dealing with an owner who has more than one property to sell.

A rolling option is really a series of options. Each time you exercise one option and buy the piece of property involved, it automatically activates the next option and ties up the next piece of property. This way you can conserve your time, energy, and money. You option the properties one at a time and you buy them one at a time, so you have time to do it all slowly. You don't get stuck taking on a bunch of different properties all at once.

For example, let's say there is a seller with seven different properties that he wants to dispose of. They are all potentially good properties, but you don't want to take all of them at once. You haven't got the time, the money, or the workmen to do it. Therefore, you want to option the properties instead. But the seller doesn't want to let you tie up all of them with options while you wait to buy them one by one. This is a perfect situation for a rolling option.

It can suit your needs and the seller's. He has the illusion that he still controls his property, while you have the security of knowing that you have it tied up, piece by piece, for when you need it. How do you pay for all of this? Well, you can try coming up with cash; if that doesn't work, for one reason or another, a lease option might.

THE LEASE OPTION

You have to give a seller valuable consideration in order to have a valid option, but that consideration doesn't have to be cash. If you lease the property, the lease can be considered payment for the option. That is a condition of your agreement to lease the property: The owner must also grant you an option to buy it.

This can benefit the seller by taking the responsibility for managing the property and leasing it off his hands. It can also benefit you by giving you control. If you are managing the property and you have a valid lease, you can keep other prospective buyers away. You can also save money this way, by not having to pay an option fee, and you get the use of the property, which you don't get with an ordinary option.

Most options give you no right to occupy the property or use it in any way until the option has been exercised. Lease options are the exception. This permits you to become familiar with the property and with all its strengths and weaknesses before you have to really commit yourself to buying it. You also get a chance to know the tenants and see which ones you want to keep and which ones you want to get rid of as soon as possible. This can be important in helping you decide which programs to apply for.

Certain tenants may help the property to qualify for certain programs, depending on their age, their financial condition, etc. Once you get to know the tenants you can find out all sorts of useful things that no set of records can tell you. In some cases, you can even apply for, and qualify for, certain federal programs just on the basis of a long-term lease. You don't even have to own the property. Control is everything, ownership is incidental.

KEY POINTS TO REMEMBER

1. Options give you the right "not" to buy the property.
2. You must offer the property-owner some valuable consideration in order to have a valid option.
3. A first-right-of-refusal option leaves you the maximum time to wheel and deal.
4. A fixed-price option protects you against inflation and rising property values.
5. A rolling option allows you to tie up several pieces of property owned by the same person. It allows you to leverage your time and money to the maximum.
6. The option should prevent the property-owner from borrowing against the property without your permission.
7. If you want the property no matter what, maybe you should buy it outright.
8. With government-assisted programs, never count on getting any money until you have it in your bank account.
9. Control is everything. Ownership is incidental, except for tax purposes.

CHAPTER SEVEN

YOUR CHECK REALLY *IS* IN THE MAIL

Why should investors care about subsidies to renters? After all, the chances are that not many of you are renters and those who are, hopefully, will be making the transition soon after reading this book and will become homeowners. So why devote an entire section to the programs available for renters? Because programs designed to help renters inevitably benefit landlords as well. The purpose of these programs is to enable low-income people to pay decent rents and get decent housing. And who supplies that decent housing? Private investors. Therefore, these programs increase the pool of available tenants, making the landlord/investor's job that much easier. In many cases they also guarantee the landlord his rents even if the tenants don't pay. In fact, in some inner-city areas, knowledgeable landlords will not even put their vacant units on the open market. They will only rent to tenants who are qualified under one of the government subsidy programs because that is the only way they can be sure of getting their rents each month. So now we're going to run through a list of these programs and see how investors can benefit from them.

RENT SUPPLEMENTS (SECTIONS 221(d)(3), 231, 236, AND 202)

HUD will pay subsidies to private landlords who own buildings insured by FHA and financed with FHA mortgages. Tenants pay up to 30% of their adjusted income and HUD pays the balance, as long as the HUD subsidy does not exceed 70% of the HUD-approved rent for the property. In other words, HUD sets maximum acceptable rents, and only landlords willing to keep their rents within those guidelines are eligible to participate.

When you deal with the government, very little is really free. Most gifts have strings attached. Of course, there is a way to get around this: HUD will only pay up to 70% of the HUD-approved rent for the property, but the tenant can make up the difference if the landlord insists on a higher rent. There is some question as to whether or not this is actually permitted under HUD rules, but the fact is, it's done all the time.

The other side of this policy is that in certain areas HUD rents are actually higher than open market rents. The reason is that HUD sets its approved rents according to features and amenities that a rental unit offers and does not really take the area into consideration. A four-bedroom two-bath apartment in the worst part of town will qualify for a higher rent than one in the best part of town if it offers features such as a washer and dryer or electric dishwasher that the other one doesn't.

HUD will subsidize the rents in any given project or property for up to 40 years. (After that time, you must tear the place down and start all over again or else find tenants who can pay their own rent.) And private nonprofit groups, limited dividend, cooperative, or other public agency sponsors who are carrying mortgages insured under any of the programs named can apply for rent supplements under this program.

Tenants must belong to low-income families that qualify for public housing and must also be elderly, handicapped, displaced by government action, victims of national disasters, occupy substandard housing; or the family must be headed by someone on active duty in the military service.

This program is being phased out and no new rent subsidies are being awarded under this program. Existing rent subsidies under Section 236 are being converted to Section 236 "deep subsidy assistance." This is another of the very specialized programs that are just not for everyone. Our next program is different.

LOWER INCOME RENTAL ASSISTANCE (SECTION 8)

This is the one! This is the program for everyone, landlords and tenants. Tenants pay either 30% of their adjusted income or 10% of their gross income, or whatever portion of their welfare allotment is supposed to go for housing, and then HUD or the local Housing Authority pays the rest, up to the maximum rent allowed under HUD or local guidelines.

The big difference is who is eligible to participate in this program: *everybody.* Nonprofit or profit-motivated developers can apply either alone or in partnership with public housing agencies. Funds provided under this program can be used for subsidizing rents in existing rental housing. Or they can be used for subsidizing rents in new construction or in properties that have been rehabbed.

HUD, or the local Housing Authority, will even help investors, builders, and developers get low interest rate loans. HUD or the local

Housing Authority then enter into a lease agreement with the property-owner for 1 year, renewable twice, with existing rental housing, and for 15 years with new construction or moderate or substantial rehabilitation projects.

APPROVED APPLICANTS

For the moderate and substantial rehabilitation projects, HUD or the local Housing Authority will even guarantee the rents for the duration of the lease. Tenants must be selected from a list of approved applicants provided by HUD or the local Housing Authority and they must be considered low-income for the area (below the midway point between the highest and lowest income group concentrations in the area). Up to 5% of the units may be rented to families whose incomes are between 50% and 80% of the median income for the area (as determined by HUD or the local Housing Authority).

The units are inspected by HUD or the local Housing Authority before a contract is signed and tenants move in. Those not matching HUD or local standards must be upgraded before they are eligible to be included in the program.

A checklist is filled out at the time tenants move in and HUD or the local Housing Authority is responsible for any damage caused by the tenants that is discovered when they leave. There is a final inspection before the tenants move out and a new checklist is filled out at that time. The landlord has a certain period of time to file for damage compensation.

Any damage beyond normal wear and tear will be charged to tenants and can affect their future eligibility for Section 8 assistance. Anyone interested in participating in this program as an investor, builder, developer, etc., has to contact his local Housing Authority or HUD office. He will be given a list of the target priorities for that area, the projects, if any, that are eligible for inclusion in the Section 8 program.

SUPPLYING THE NEED

HUD or the Housing Authority might, for example, decide that there is a need in one area for 100 units of two-bedroom rental housing and 75 units of three-bedroom rental housing. They will put up notices to that effect and accept bids from builders and developers with projects they would like to include in the Section 8 program. These can be properties that the investor, builder, or developer already owns or properties they would like to buy, as long as they fit the guidelines.

Once the quota for two- and three-bedroom units has been filled, no more applications or bids will be accepted. Think about the opportunities and possibilities these programs offer: You can get assistance in financing the purchase of the property, often at below-market interest rates. You can have your rents guaranteed, with automatic increases every year, for the next 15 years!

If a tenant moves out and the Housing Authority or HUD has no suitable tenants to move in right away, you still get paid. And by buying property in run-down or undervalued areas, you can even get above-market rents. A lot of people are making a lot of money with this one and a lot of tenants are getting decent housing they could never afford on their own.

Elderly or disabled people can get special consideration under Section 8 assistance, and there are special programs to encourage builders and developers to build housing for the elderly and disabled.

FARMERS HOME ADMINISTRATION (FMHA)
RURAL RENTER ASSISTANCE PROGRAMS

In addition to the programs offered by HUD and its subsidiary, FHA, there are programs specifically aimed at low- and moderate-income families living in country areas and in towns of less than 20,000 people through the Farmers Home Administration (FmHA) of the U.S. Department of Agriculture.

FmHA makes loans to help profit-motivated investors, builders, and developers, as well as nonprofit organizations, build inexpensive rental housing in rural areas and, in some cases, FmHA also regulates the rents to keep them affordable. These programs are similar to HUD/FHA programs designed to stimulate construction of low-income housing, but they don't really overlap. FmHA is part of an entirely different branch of the U.S. government (the Department of Agriculture) with different ideas, goals, and a different mandate than HUD/FHA.

The Department of Housing and Urban Development is specifically set up to deal with the housing needs of people in urban areas, while the Department of Agriculture is concerned with the overall problems of people in rural areas, not just their housing needs. This means that FmHA has different standards and priorities, specifically suited to the areas in which it operates.

RURAL AREAS ARE MORE STABLE AND HOMOGENEOUS. In rural areas, families tend to be larger and stay together longer. Children are not as likely to move out and get their own place to live as soon as they are grown. There are fewer singles and transients floating in and out of the area in search of housing. Therefore, housing needs in rural areas must

109

be more specifically pinpointed and related to the needs of the community-at-large.

This can be a sensitive question, particularly in areas that wish to maintain their rural or small-town atmosphere. For this reason, FmHA guidelines specifically call for projects to be aesthetically designed, to allow for maximum open space, and to blend into the environment as much as possible.

The FmHA-subsidized housing program is a community-oriented program, with the emphasis on rural communities and their preservation, not urbanization. For this reason, it is even more important than it is with HUD/FHA programs to submit a clear plan stating the benefits to the community and documenting the need for the project. You can't expect to go in there and build whatever you want and then get FmHA funding just because you're willing to offer some of the units to low-income tenants. It just doesn't work that way.

You have to submit all your plans in advance and have them approved. FmHA works with local lenders and local community advisory boards to determine which programs are really necessary for the community and have a good chance for success. They want projects that will strengthen local communities, not just enrich developers and bring in outsiders.

Areas that have a traditional shortage of affordable housing for the existing residents or areas that are going through a natural period of growth and expansion (due to creation of new jobs or business opportunities) are the natural targets for these programs, along with rural areas where the existing housing is decaying and in need of replacement. Commuter developments designed to turn rural areas into suburbs and bedroom communities for nearby cities will generally not qualify. They usually fall under the jurisdiction of HUD/FHA instead.

Wrap-up and Recap of Government Programs for Renters

Now it's time to go back through the options for renters who would like some assistance from the government. There are not many of them listed here simply because most of the available choices are covered by two basic programs: The Section 8 program, run by HUD (the Department of Housing and Urban Development), and the Farmers Home Administration Rural Renter Assistance program for people in towns with less than 20,000 people and country areas, run by FmHA (the Farmers Home Administration) of the Department of Agriculture.

Both of these government departments have programs that give special preference to builders of housing for the elderly or disabled as well as subsidized housing programs for families of low or moderate incomes. For details, you have to check with your local HUD/FHA or FmHA office, since availability of programs depends upon how much demand there is at the local level. Many areas have filled their quotas for various programs and have long waiting lists of eligible renters waiting to join.

For example, a given area may have a goal or quota of 300 units of elderly housing for that fiscal year. Once that quota is filled and contracts have been signed for those 300 units, the program is closed for the rest of that fiscal year. There may very well be more than 300 elderly people approved and waiting for subsidized housing, but the rest will just have to wait.

On the other hand, there may also be a goal of 100 units of special housing made accessible for the handicapped and that goal may be unfilled. Therefore, you would be wasting your time submitting a proposal for elderly housing; but if you made your property wheelchair-accessible or did whatever else was required to turn it into approved housing for the handicapped, then you might be eligible for guaranteed rents, low-cost financing, and other benefits as well.

111

Just remember, you have to adapt, the government doesn't. If there is a conflict between what you have or propose and what HUD or the local Housing Authority decides is needed, then you are the one who is going to have to change your plans. Check with your local Housing Authority or the local HUD or FmHA office before you buy the property and start working on it. Find out what funds are allocated for subsidizing housing and what the requirements are for participating in the various programs that are available.

KEY POINTS TO REMEMBER

1. **Programs designed to help renters inevitably benefit landlords as well.**

2. **In some inner-city areas, knowledgeable landlords will only rent to tenants qualified under one of the government subsidy programs, to insure receiving rents each month.**

3. **HUD decides upon the quotas to be set for housing units based upon need.**

4. **FmHA Rural Renter Assistance programs are aimed at low- and moderate-income families living in towns and rural areas of less than 20,000 people.**

CHAPTER EIGHT

LOW PAYMENTS, HIGH INCOME

IT WORKS ALL OVER THE COUNTRY

My graduates are successfully using government programs (particularly the Section 8 subsidized rent program) in the East, the West, and everywhere in between. You don't have to be Al Lowry to make these programs work and you don't have to jump in and start with multimillion-dollar projects either. *You can start as small as you like* and work your way up, if and when you feel comfortable doing it. Or you can even stay small and keep your real estate investments strictly a part-time venture, while you pursue your other interests. The government is there to work with you and help you either way.

Right in my own backyard, in Oakland, California, where I got started, my graduates have been using government programs in a variety of ways, both for rehab projects and for long-term rentals.

A True Success Story

One of my graduates is a young man named Brian Wong who had failed in four attempts to become a real estate agent. He thought that was the way to make money, since most real estate agents seemed to drive expensive cars and wear nice clothes. The only problem was that he couldn't pass the test. He was ready to give up and forget about real estate. Then he attended a free lecture that I gave and took my weekend seminar. He walked out of the seminar determined to make it as an investor, even if he couldn't make it as a real estate agent. He began looking for properties and attending the local Lowry alumni group. Brian's goal was to quit his job as an insurance salesman and get into real estate full-time. He thought he could do it within three to five years. He was wrong. It took him only two years.

Oakland is generally considered to be a tough place in which to be a landlord these days. It is a desirable location, right across the bay from San Francisco, the highest-priced housing market in the country. As such, real estate prices are high and there is a lot of competition from homebuyers who will pay more than investors will, especially for single-family homes and small apartment buildings up to four units. Therefore, most beginning investors can only afford to buy property in the worst areas.

The tenant problems alone are bad enough to scare off many people, but most investors have to put up with negative cash flow as well. It can be awfully discouraging to take money out of your pocket each month to support a property that gives you trouble.

Who's Afraid of the Big, Bad Tenants?

Eliminating tenant problems is the first step. I teach part-time, hands-off management techniques in my seminar and in my book, *How to Manage Real Estate Successfully—In Your Spare Time* (Simon and Schuster), so my graduates have an automatic advantage over others. Brian Wong learned what type of tenants to look for and what type to avoid, and how the Section 8 subsidized rent program makes it even easier to pick good tenants.

But eliminating tenant problems isn't enough. That's like the man with two rocks in his shoe who removes one and then tries to run a marathon. You don't become financially independent that way. What you want everyone wants: properties that will bring in income, not properties that eat up the income you have. It's not easy.

Getting Good Rents in Bad Areas

Section 8 pays higher than market rents in many areas. This is because the government doesn't take the neighborhood or the property value into account when they set rent levels. Rent levels are set on a city- or area-wide basis. They are determined on the basis of size of the living area and amenities offered. A three-bedroom apartment with wall-to-wall carpet, central heat, and built-in appliances will rent for the same amount no matter where it is located. It can be in the best part of town or the worst part of town; the rent will be the same.

115

This means it doesn't make much sense for owners in good neighborhoods to lease their properties under the Section 8 program and it doesn't make sense for landlords in bad neighborhoods to do anything else. An apartment that will rent for $550 a month with Section 8 guarantees and rent subsidies might rent for $750 or $800 a month on the open market. Or it might rent for $400 or less. It all depends on where it is located. Once Brian Wong realized this, it took him less than three years to become financially independent and less than six months to quit his job and go into real estate full-time.

Someone at a Lowry alumni meeting suggested that he become a real estate appraiser, since appraisers don't have to be licensed in California and he could get to see a lot of properties that way. So Brian got himself into a training program for appraisers run by a local savings and loan association and then was hired as a staff appraiser when he finished the training program.

Soon he was familiar with the entire city of Oakland and most of the surrounding area for a 50-mile radius. He knew the good areas and he knew the bad areas. He learned what the average prices were, so he knew when he ran across a bargain. Soon, he found himself making offers on properties he was sent to appraise and buying them himself.

Brian also learned what the average rents were in most areas, because that was part of his job. He had to appraise income properties and, in order to do that, he had to know what the income was and how that corresponded with the property value.

The private rental market is risky in many areas. Brian saw many properties that were either trashed or just plain run down by the tenants and others, that were going into foreclosure because the owners couldn't collect the rents. Section 8 properties—those where the tenants were registered with the Section 8 program—seemed to have higher rents and less wear and tear and fewer tenant problems.

FHA and VA loans were fully assumable, even when they carried very low interest rates; FHA and VA repos were available at favorable terms. It didn't take Brian long to realize that there was a lot the government could do for him to make it easier for him to buy property.

Less Than $1,000 to Start

When he started, Brian had less than $1,000. It was a big decision for him to take my seminar, since he had a wife and four small daughters to support. He never made more than $2,000 a month as an appraiser, but within three years, Brian had bought several million dollars worth of property, mostly apartment buildings of four to ten units. A positive cash flow of $9,000 a month was enough to make Brian Wong quit his job and become a full-time investor. It took him a little more than two and a half years to get there.

Within another year, Brian got bored being in semi-retirement, so he opened his own company as an independent real estate appraiser. Being out in the field looking at property got him stimulated and he started buying property again. Only this time he had the money to get into some bigger projects with even bigger profits. He found one building that he appraised for $1.4 million. He bought it for the full price, using proven methods that he learned in the Lowry seminar, so he didn't have to put up any of his own money, and then started rooting out the problem tenants and replacing them, mostly with people who were qualified for Section 8. A year later, as soon as the holding period for long-term capital gains had passed, he sold the building for $1.8 million, a $400,000 profit, and exchanged his way into something even larger.

Brian Wong may be unusually successful, but he isn't alone. The Oakland area is full of Lowry success stories, like Jim and Peggy Carver, my ex-handyman and his wife, who now own about $8 million worth of real estate and live in a $350,000 house; and Simon Lantzer, who became a part-time real estate millionaire while running a full-time electronics business (and making it grow). Brian Wong isn't the only one getting rich with Section 8 rents.

You Can Do It Wherever You Live

Low payments and high rents equal positive cash flow. When you buy properties in the poor areas of town, you get low payments. First, you pay less for the property, and second, you can force more concessions from sellers, because they are more anxious to get rid of their properties.

You don't have to be in a glamorous, high-priced market to do it, either. Two of my graduates, Wayne Phillips in Baltimore and Don Gibson in Cleveland, have proven that this is an excellent way to make money, no matter where you are located. Wayne calls himself the "Multi-Unit King" and, at last count, owned or controlled over 500 units, most of them purchased with low-interest government-subsidized loans and then leased out to tenants covered under Section 8 or other government programs. Don Gibson doesn't have nearly as many units—something less than 200—but he's found ways to pull out large amounts of tax-free cash every time he closes a deal.

All of these people would have made it on their own, without the government's help. They are all determined and highly motivated people and they are all Lowry graduates, with all the tools they need to succeed as real estate investors. But each has been able to buy properties for next to nothing, because these properties were located in areas where most people were afraid to buy. They were able to invest money in these properties, knowing they would get the money back in the form of increased rents. They wouldn't be overimproving the properties.

Section 8 guarantees investors a profit by creating value out of nothing. This is no accident. It's a conscious policy and one that works very well. When investors know they can go into poor neighborhoods and make a reasonable profit with minimal risk, they will do it. If they know they will make money by spending money, they will maintain their properties and even improve them. By guaranteeing the rents, the

118

Section 8 program offers investors the security they need. Many deteriorating neighborhoods are saved in this way and restored to prosperity, while the property owners in the area become prosperous as well.

The "Multi-Unit King" of Baltimore

Take Wayne Phillips, for example. He wanted to get into real estate in a big way and make a lot of money. He was willing to put a lot of time and work into it (as long as it didn't require any money, because he didn't have any). He was a starving musician, but he found a way to get fat with subsidized rents.

MULTIPLE LISTINGS MEAN MULTIPLE OPPORTUNITIES and that's where Wayne started. He went through the Multiple Listing and started making offers, over 500 of them in one year. Of course, he didn't go to see all of those properties. That would have been physically impossible. He had no desire to see all of those properties, no need to physically inspect them until he knew that his offers were going to be accepted. He just put a clause into each offer making it contingent upon his inspection and approval of the property, if and when the seller accepted.

A lot of real estate agents got furious, but Wayne knew he was dealing ultimately with the property-owners, not the agents, so he didn't care. He recognized that any sellers who were serious about getting rid of their properties would at least counter his offers, no matter what their agents thought, so he kept sending them out on a regular basis.

All he cared about were the numbers. Some properties made sense only if there were assumable low-interest loans or the seller was willing

119

to carry at least part of the financing. Other properties were good bets for all cash, low price offers. The important thing was that he knew he would have no trouble filling all the properties he bought with good tenants and he could predict exactly what the income would be for each property.

TITLE I LOANS PROVIDE EASY-ACCESS CASH and Wayne used this cash to improve his properties, his cash flow, and his net worth. He wound up buying over 100 properties that first year out of the 500 offers he made. Many of them required fix-up work, but Wayne wasn't worried about that. He had his own crew do the work and with Title I loans to provide the money—up to $7,500 per unit—there was no stopping him. Not even an excess of tax shelter could slow him down, so he says.

SELLING UNNEEDED TAX SHELTER FOR EXTRA PROFITS was the next logical step, once Wayne had his own needs covered and his own taxes down to zero. He began forming limited partnerships and giving most of the tax benefits to the limited partners, right up to the limit that the law allows.

He was able to raise a lot of cash this way and he didn't have to give the limited partners nearly as much for the profits. With the cash from his limited partners he was able to buy more property and get into bigger projects, projects designed for the elderly, that generated even more investors. Today, Wayne Phillips is no longer a starving musician. He is a wealthy man.

THE "CASH-BACK KING" OF CLEVELAND

Don Gibson was already on his way to becoming wealthy when he took my seminar. He had a successful business designing dress patterns for hard-to-fit women and he was making lots of money. His only interest in real estate was as a part-time side venture, nothing serious. But once he took my seminar and realized the opportunities out there, he got so excited that he left $250,000 worth of dress patterns sitting in a warehouse.

He walked away from his business and went into real estate investing full time. He's never looked back since. He buys property in the worst areas of Cleveland from battle-scarred landlords who can't wait to get away. Like Brian Wong in California, he finds people who have tenant problems, people in default or foreclosure, or just over the edge with frustration. These people are so anxious to sell and so afraid that they'll never find a buyer that they sell their properties for far less than they're worth, just to be rid of the burden of ownership.

Don gets them to transfer title to him first and then to agree to wait up to 60 days to get the purchase price in cash. Sixty days seems like a long time to them, but the waiting isn't nearly as bad if they can be absolved of all responsibility for the property in the meantime. Once Don has the title in his name, he goes out and refinances the property and pulls out tax-free cash.

Pay $60,000 for a property and borrow $90,000 against it. That's Don's style of investing. For example, Don will agree to buy a building for $60,000, get the owner to sign the title over to him, and then go out and get the building appraised at $150,000 and put a 60% loan on the property for $90,000. He gives the seller $60,000 in cash (minus the amount of any existing liens against the property) and pockets the other $30,000, tax-free. Why tax-free? Because it's borrowed money.

121

It's not income, therefore it's not taxable. As far as the IRS is concerned, it's not Don's money.

The only thing that is taxable is the $200 to $300 a month he usually gets in positive cash flow after he's refinanced the property. Even at the depth of the recession, when mortgage rates hit 18% and higher, Don was able to pull out cash this way and still maintain a positive cash flow. The properties he buys are so underpriced in relation to their potential income that he can get positive cash flow and pull out tax-free cash too. That's how much positive cash flow the previous owners are willing to walk away from.

Why do they do this? Why would anyone sell a $150,000 property for $60,000? Fear, plain and simple, fear of coming into the neighborhood, fear of trying to collect the rents and deal with the tenants. Fear of what the tenants, or outside vandals, will eventually do to the property. These are the main motives Don encounters in the people he deals with.

Many have inherited their properties from ancestors who bought or built them when the neighborhoods were better, quite different from today. They feel times have changed and it's time to get out. They really have nothing invested in their properties, financially or emotionally, so anything they can get out of them in a hurry is usually good enough.

Don takes over, kicks out the bad tenants, and does whatever needs to be done to get the property back into shape. If all the tenants are bad, he evicts the worst ones first and hopes that will scare all the others into line, at least for a little while. Gradually, he gets the whole building cleaned out and leased to people who qualify for Section 8. Then, his positive cash flow increases even more. He finds he has almost no problems with the tenants who are on Section 8. All across the country, the story is the same: Section 8 tenants can't afford to cause trouble because they don't want to lose their eligibility.

It's a Landlords' Market

Many landlords won't deal with Section 8 because they don't want to deal with the government bureaucracy, or because they think they can get more on the open market. This puts more pressure on tenants who want to use Section 8. Since some landlords won't rent to them, they have to be nice to those who will. Having Section 8 eligibility doesn't guarantee them a place to live. They still have to go out and find a house or apartment on their own and convince the landlord to rent to them. If they are a nuisance, the landlord doesn't even have to evict them. All he has to do is refuse to renew their lease when it expires.

Don Gibson has used this principle to acquire and successfully manage more than a hundred units in Cleveland. Wayne Phillips has done it in Baltimore and Brian Wong has done it in Oakland. But you don't have to think big to make it big with Section 8; you can do it with just a few single-family houses too. Simon Lantzer did it in Oakland, California, and Douglas Stephen is doing it in Tucson, Arizona.

You Don't Have to be a Full-Time Investor to Succeed. You can put in as much or as little time as you want. These programs are meant for the little guy as well as the big guy. As long as you're willing to get out there and try to do something to improve your life by improving housing opportunities for other people, there are programs to help you do it.

Albert Lowry

A MILLIONAIRE AT NINETEEN (HOUSES)

Like Don Gibson, Simon Lantzer had other interests and a successful career outside of real estate. He also took my seminar with the idea of getting into real estate as a sideline. He was a highly trained electrical engineer who had spent years preparing himself and was advancing within his chosen profession. He had no intention of giving it up and making a career change to go into real estate. He just wanted to get a few houses, fix them up, and manage them in his spare time, so he could have some extra income and tax shelter and build up his net worth.

Of course, I told him about another engineer who started out that way, buying and fixing up real estate in his spare time, and who wound up owning a $10 million Hollywood mansion and the Los Angeles Lakers basketball team. But Simon Lantzer is not Jerry Buss. He had his own ideas and his own ambitions. He didn't want to get nearly that involved with real estate. He wanted to keep it a small part of his life.

At first, he wasn't even sure that he wanted to get involved in real estate at all, once he saw what was out there and what he was able to afford. It was a scary prospect and he had his doubts.

MANY BEGINNING INVESTORS' ONLY EXPERIENCE IS WITH THEIR OWN HOUSE and this was the case with Simon Lantzer. He had lived all of his life in rented apartments, until he got married and he and his wife bought a little two-bedroom house for $35,000, using their entire savings for the down payment. A few years later, they sold it for $65,000 when they decided they needed a bigger house. Simon learned something from the experience. He realized that there was no way he could have afforded the new house without the equity he had built up

124

in the first one. He began to appreciate the potential power of real estate as an investment. If he had made so much money on a house that he had bought just to live in, he began to wonder what he could do if he invested his money in real estate with the idea of making a profit.

That was what led him to my seminar, but he still had a lot of obstacles to overcome, mainly his own fear. By this time, Simon was doing well for himself as an engineer and he and his family lived in a big house on a large, secluded lot in a wealthy suburb. Naturally, this was also the type of property he saw himself owning as an investor, until he quickly realized that he could never afford it.

First, he didn't have any large reserve of equity to draw on this time, since he had no intention of selling his house, so he couldn't afford the down payment necessary to buy expensive property in the suburbs. Second, he found that even if he could afford to buy another house similar to the one he lived in, he could never afford to keep it. The rents wouldn't cover the payments.

Simon made a good living as an engineer, but with a wife and two young children, he spent it all too. This was why he wanted to get into real estate. He saw it as the only way to build up his net worth and have something someday when he was ready to retire. There was no way he could afford to support any property that wouldn't support itself.

Unfortunately, this meant Simon had to forget about investing in his own backyard and look toward the city. He knew he didn't want to live there. He had worked long and hard to get away from the city to where he was living now. The question was whether anyone else still wanted to live in the city and whether it was safe for him to invest there. The more he began to investigate, the bleaker his prospects looked. Even in the city, he couldn't afford to invest in any of the areas that he considered decent or safe. They were still priced out of his reach.

Oakland was considered reasonably priced compared to San Francisco across the bay, but it was still one of the highest-priced real estate markets in the country. Simon soon realized that the only way he could afford to buy any property at all was to go to the heart of the ghetto, an area he had never even been to and had no real desire to visit. Oakland had a nasty reputation. It was the birthplace of both the Black Panthers and the Hell's Angels, neither one of which would appear on the average landlord's list of favorite groups to rent to. Simon was well aware of this as he began looking for properties.

THE WORSE THE AREA IS, THE MORE INCOME YOU GET for the same purchase price. It didn't take Simon too long to figure that out. The houses that were selling for $100,000 and up in his nice, safe attractive suburban community might rent for $750 a month. In Oakland, he could buy houses for $20,000 that would rent for $450 a month. He could get more income each month by owning only $40,000 worth of property.

The only problem was that this was all on paper. In reality, Simon was afraid he would never collect his rents, and that he would have all sorts of maintenance problems and evictions. He didn't want to lose money and he didn't want to spend all of his time dealing with real estate.

SECTION 8 PAYS FOR TENANT-CAUSED DAMAGES and Simon overcame most of his fears, once he found out about the Section 8 program and what it could do for him. When Simon realized that the rents were guaranteed, he felt almost safe, but not quite.

In many cases, when he went to look at a house, the neighborhood seemed very bad to him. But he didn't really have to worry about buying property in areas like that, because the government would reimburse him for any damage. It took a little while for this to really sink in. Simon had trouble believing that Section 8 would really do all it was supposed to do. He's a cautious, conservative type of person and he wanted to be sure. He began by buying one house, fixing it up himself, and then renting it out to a single woman who qualified for Section 8 rent subsidies.

He did minimal work to the house—mostly painting and cleaning—and then rented it for a nice, positive cash flow. Each month, he received his rent like clockwork, just before the first of the month. The tenant never gave him any trouble and everything seemed to work out fine, so he went ahead and bought another house. His plan was to buy a house a year for five years and expand slowly. He expected it would be at least five years before he could really afford to improve his style of living, but plans don't always work out exactly as we expect them to.

Simon would up buying nineteen houses within the next three years and becoming a millionaire in the process. With an average monthly cash flow of $300 per house, he had a comfortable enough income so that he could have retired, but instead, he decided to open his own business. He used the equity in his real estate as collateral for loans and the positive cash flow to make the loan payments until his business got off the ground and became self-supporting.

Today, he owns million-dollar equities in his real estate and his electronics business, but he still owns less than twenty houses. Everybody's got to do things his own way.

FROM HANDYMAN TO LANDLORD

Jim and Peggy Carver worked their way up from the bottom, the same way that my wife and I did, with a lot of hard work, guts, and determination. When we decided to leave Oakland and move up to Lake Tahoe, we sold the Carvers a lot of our properties, all the small ones that were too hard to manage long-distance. From there, they took off on their own, becoming experts on handling tenants in the Oakland housing market and learning about all the different programs HUD and the local Housing Authority had available and figuring out how to use them to best advantage. They have prospered as a result.

127

A LANDLORD'S MISTAKE

Without the government, you're all alone; it can be a lonely feeling being a landlord, particularly in a marginal neighborhood. Someone I know recently found this out the hard way. He had a duplex in a borderline neighborhood and for years had it comfortably rented under the Section 8 program. Then he got cocky.

He didn't like his tenant, so he decided to get rid of her. He had no grounds for evicting her, but he decided not to renew her lease at the end of the year. She always paid her rent on time and she kept up her apartment, but she was nasty and argumentative. She fought with the other tenants. She fought with my friend and did her best to harass him.

He had rented to her partially because she had a teenage son who lived with her. He thought they would be good, trouble-free tenants. The son wouldn't have any wild parties because he was living with his mother and the mother wouldn't have any parties because she was living with her son. The son was a big, strong boy and my friend assumed that he would take care of any maintenance, such as fixing minor leaks, etc.

The first assumption worked out. The second one didn't. There were no loud parties, but there were loud, screaming phone calls every time there was any minor problem. The son was a lazy slob and wouldn't lift a finger to do anything around the house, so his mother expected my friend to be at her beck and call. Finally, he had enough. He decided to see if he could get a better tenant, one who wouldn't be so unpleasant to deal with.

SOMETIMES RENTS IN IMPROVING NEIGHBORHOODS RISE FASTER THAN SECTION 8 WILL ALLOW. This is what happened in my friend's case. He could have been rid of her and gotten another Section 8 tenant, but he felt that the neighborhood had improved and that he could get more rent on the open market. So he waited until her lease was up and then refused to renew it. He refused to take any other Section 8 tenants and he put the property on the open market.

He got another single mother with a teenage son as a tenant (some people get fixated on an idea and find it hard to drop), and this time he spelled it out, right in the rental agreement, that they were to be responsible for all minor maintenance themselves. He went over the rental agreement with them, line by line, and made sure that they understood this part and agreed to it. He even had them initial that section.

All of her references checked out perfectly; everything went fine for the first month. Then, he didn't get the rent. He went to see his new tenant and she gave him $100 and a great sob story. He waited another month before he started eviction proceedings; then she hit him with an even better story, the oldest one in the book: "Your check's in the mail." She even gave him the serial numbers for the two money orders she had supposedly sent him. He waited another couple of weeks before he filed to evict her again and it was another month after that before he got her out.

He hired a crew and cleaned the whole place, top to bottom, and got it ready to rent again. The night it was done, someone broke in and started a fire.

My friend couldn't prove anything, but he was awfully suspicious, especially when his ex-tenant showed up the day after the fire to visit a friend next door. If the property had been rented under the Section 8 program, he would have been able to get at least enough money to cover the rent he had lost, if not the fire damage.

Now, of course, I'm not saying that this will happen to you if you try to rent your properties on the open market. But it is an all-too-frequent type of occurrence in certain areas and many beginning investors get themselves into trouble buying cheap properties in areas they are not really prepared to deal with, but it doesn't have to be that way.

Rehab Riches in the Desert

The 203K program offers rehab riches and Douglas Stephen is cashing in on them. He buys properties in the poorer areas of town, because that's where they're cheapest and most in need of rehabilitation. He buys up those mistakes that the beginning investors made and gets low-cost government financing to buy and rehab them.

He gets in with little of his own money and then pulls cash out by getting the rehabbing work done for less than the amount of money he is allotted for the job. In this way, he is able to do something positive for his community and put money in his own pocket besides. He does an honest job restoring the properties and he earns an honest profit for it.

BEING AN APPROVED SUBCONTRACTOR is a great way to increase those profits and Doug has that angle covered too. He plows his positive cash flow back into real estate and related businesses. He's a partner in a roofing company, a general contractor, and owns a pest control company.

Now, who do you think gets all of his and most of his clients' roofing, termite, and general contracting work? He creates work for himself and his own companies and he helps the economy of Tucson's worst areas as well. He employs local people who would be unemployed otherwise and gives them a chance to learn valuable skills and, as long as he can keep buying properties and having the government fund the whole operation, he can keep them all working steadily.

There are government programs designed to help you, no matter who you are or what your goals are, from buying a home of your own to multimillion-dollar apartment complexes. The government has a range of programs much too broad to be covered in just one chapter. It's going to take the rest of the book to go through them and explain how they might relate to you. So, if you'll turn the page, we'll start with how Uncle Sam can make you wealthy. . . .

KEY POINTS TO REMEMBER

1. **Section 8 rent guarantees can make bad areas safe for landlords.**
2. **Section 8 protects landlords against any damage caused by the tenants.**
3. **Section 8 rents are set on a city- or area-wide basis with no regard to neighborhoods.**
4. **In poor areas, you get more income for the same purchase price.**
5. **In poor areas, you get more concessions from sellers.**

CHAPTER NINE

HOW UNCLE SAM CAN MAKE YOU WEALTHY

HELP FOR THOSE WHO HELP OTHERS

Uncle Sam helps those who help others and Uncle Sam will help you become rich if you help low-income people solve their housing problems. It has become very fashionable today to knock the government and talk about all of its failures, what it's not doing for everyone. Even the President is constantly talking about cutting the size of government. It's easy to forget or overlook all the good things that government does do.

I'm partial to government programs myself, because they helped to make me a very wealthy man when I was just getting my start in real estate. At one time, when I was building my real estate, I was one of the largest landlords involved with government-subsidized low- and moderate-income housing in Oakland, California.

This is not to imply that I wouldn't have become successful at real estate investing without government programs, because that's not so. Once I learned the principles of using other people's money to buy well-selected investment real estate and then using it as a vehicle for creating wealth, nothing could have stopped me. But having the government as an ally made it easier.

A Fortune Is Waiting

A million-dollar hidden fortune in real estate is waiting for you. My wife and I started out buying mostly foreclosure properties, because those were the cheapest properties available and they offered the most opportunity for making a profit. We found that we could buy them for 50 cents or 60 cents on the dollar, fix them up with a little bit of ingenuity and hard work, and make big profits.

The only problem was that a lot of them were in bad neighborhoods and suffered from vandalism and other tenant problems. In many cases, this was why they had gone into foreclosure in the first place. My wife and I quickly realized that, unless we could figure out a way to solve these problems, we would be no better off than the previous owners. All of our hard work and money would be wasted if the properties kept getting trashed or we couldn't collect the rents.

We started making inquiries to find out what successful landlords did in these neighborhoods, and that's how we found out about the Housing Authority and the Section 8 program for low-income renters. We found that leasing to the Housing Authority was the only way to be a landlord in bad neighborhoods, and bad neighborhoods were the only ones we could really afford when we were starting out. The

Housing Authority not only guaranteed that we would get our rents, it also guaranteed to reimburse us for any damage the tenants might cause. Not only that but, in many cases, the rents that the Housing Authority paid were higher than what we could get on the open market, and the Housing Authority or some other government agency, such as the local HUD office or the city's Rediscovery Agency, helped us obtain financing.

CONTRACTORS MAKE MORE MONEY

Extra profit as a government-approved contractor was the next logical step. This got us into building turnkey housing projects, which we sold to the Housing Authority once they were completed. This arrangement provided good housing for low-income tenants and profits for us.

The government pays all expenses. I was also able to charge the government for my overhead as a contractor: office expenses, secretarial help, etc. These are expenses I would have to absorb on my own as an investor, but as long as I was a government-approved contractor, Uncle Sam picked up the tab. I was in business as a contractor and HUD wanted to make sure that I made a profit. All of this was just gravy. The real meat and potatoes didn't come until the project was completed. That's where the big money was waiting. As a contractor, I was able to make a lot of money, but as a shrewd investor, I was able to make a lot more money, and really profit from the work I did as a contractor, once the job was finished. That was when I got my real payoff for a job well done: Section 8 long-term leases with guaranteed rents.

The government is your customer when you are trying to do government-approved rehab projects. And the customer is always right. Therefore, if you want to succeed, you have to know what the government wants and how to create it. This is where a lot of investors go wrong. They get scared off by the idea of dealing with the government bureaucracy. They think it will be too difficult. In reality, dealing with the bureaucracy is not difficult at all, once you know what you're doing. It takes a little patience and persistence, but it's really not so very hard to do. Most people exaggerate the difficulties and forget one important fact: The government is a more than willing and eager buyer. Once the government identifies certain housing needs in a given area, the government is eager to deal with responsible investors and contractors who can help fill that need. But that's the key: You've got to know what the needs are before you can fill them. Don't get the government's priorities confused with your own.

Government housing subsidies are meant to help renters. They are not specifically designed to benefit investors, although that's the main side effect they produce. The main goal is to help prospective renters who are in need of housing. So that's where you have to start.

You can't just pick any property at random, decide that you are going to rehabilitate it, or build on it and get government money to do the job. Unfortunately, it doesn't work quite that way. You have to get approval in advance and the government must determine that there is a need for the type of housing you want to create.

The government sets goals and quotas for each area and then solicits bids and proposals from interested investors and contractors. For example, they may decide that there is a need for 100 two-bedroom apartments and 300 three-bedroom apartments for the next fiscal year and they will fund only projects involving two- and three-bedroom apartments. If you have a building full of one-bedroom apartments or four-bedroom apartments, you are out of luck. If your building contains two-bedroom apartments but plans have already been accepted for the renovation of 100 or more two-bedroom apartments, you are out until at least the next fiscal year.

The only way to work with the government is to check on the local priorities first. Find out what's needed and what's being funded before you jump in and buy the property and start doing the work. See if there is any way you can modify your original plans to conform better to what the local authorities want and are prepared to fund.

Today, my wife and I have money, lots of it, and so we don't have to buy problem properties in bad neighborhoods anymore. We are able to buy property in any area, including the most exclusive. But we haven't forgotten the way we got rich in the first place. And we are still using the same techniques and the same programs to make money today.

We are still buying foreclosures and still fixing them up and leasing them to the government. In fact, we recently made a half million dollars in tax-free cash, plus a considerable amount of equity on just one transaction, with the government's help. The whole deal was supposed to be a loss for us but, instead, we turned it around and made a healthy profit. Who could pass that up? It was easy for us because we knew what to do. We know how helpful the government can be.

PROFITING FROM ADVERSITY

It all started with a foreclosure on two adjacent properties in Oakland, California. Our own. We had previously bought the buildings and then sold them, but the owners had defaulted, so we had to take them back. The buildings were now run down and filled with disreputable types who earned their rent money, when they earned it and paid it at all, in a variety of illegal ways. The good tenants, the families and hard-working people who wanted a decent place to live, were trapped. Oakland has a housing shortage and most tenants had little or no money to move, anyway. They were paying their rent but there weren't enough of them.

First, we had to foreclose on one building and then, shortly after that, we had to foreclose on the second one too. The buildings were hell holes. They had started life as nice, middle-class housing—the larger building even had a swimming pool—but neglect and a deteriorating neighborhood had gradually done them in. They seemed to be barely worth saving.

The neighborhood was improving, but it seemed to be too late for the buildings. Some of the apartments were literally gutted. Drug addicts and other thieves had stolen everything of value, including sinks, bathtubs, wash basins and fixtures, carpets and drapes, stoves and refrigerators. There were big holes punched in the doors, the walls, the ceilings; graffiti were everywhere, even on the sidewalks around the buildings. Everyone in the neighborhood seemed to go through the unfenced courtyard of the larger building as a shortcut to the next street. With all those people passing through all the time, no one knew who belonged on the property and who didn't. There were always strangers hanging around and there were constant burglaries.

We had really goofed when we sold the properties. The buyers looked good on paper, so we had agreed to carry the financing. But the buyers turned out to be totally unreliable and untrustworthy. By the time we took the properties back, they weren't worth very much anymore because they had so many problems. The situation was so bad that most people felt that the only value left, at that point, was in the land, and it would just cost money to tear the buildings down. But I had worked with the government before and so I was well aware of the possibilities for rehabilitating the properties, making them useful and productive again, and then leasing them to the local Housing Authority at a profit.

REHABILITATION TAX WRITE-OFFS

The government gives investors special tax breaks for rehabilitating properties and renting the units to approved low-income tenants. We knew we could get either a dollar-for-dollar tax credit or a special accelerated depreciation schedule if the properties were at least thirty years old and HUD or the Housing Authority approved. Unfortunately, these properties were too new to qualify for those special tax breaks; however, the combination of benefits that was available was almost irresistible. Where other people saw a double disaster, I saw a double opportunity. The area was improving and there was no shortage of potential tenants, especially with the government to help pay their rent. Therefore, I was confident that it would be a profitable venture, even though the properties had been so thoroughly and totally trashed. Besides, I didn't have too many other choices. I was stuck with the properties, for better or worse, so I could either use them as a tax loss or try to find some way to turn a profit on them.

Low risk meant high returns. I was even more confident, since I knew that I wouldn't have to put much of my own money into the project. I knew I could finance most, if not all, of the necessary rehabilitation and then I could rent the renovated units under the Section 8 program, so my risk would be minimal. The less I had to risk, the more the project made sense to me. The less I had to invest, the higher my return would be. This is the type of investment I like.

If I leverage my money, putting only a little bit into each investment, I can make it go a lot further and spread it out among several different investments. This way, I get more appreciation, more positive cash flow when rents start going up, and more tax shelter. Get all the benefits that real estate can provide, that's my philosophy of investing. I make sure that I get the most benefit from the least amount of money.

Government-subsidized housing makes it easy to do. When you buy foreclosure properties for a fraction of their true value and then rent them safely, with rents guaranteed by the government, it gives you an automatic advantage over other investors who are paying full market rates. You get to keep more of the income from the property, so you can do more with the property. You can attract better tenants than you might normally be able to get. Once you understand the full use of leverage and selective investing, it can have all sorts of unexpected benefits.

Higher Rents and Bigger Profits

The government helped me raise my rents. First of all, by subsidizing rents, the government increased the pool of available tenants. Think about it for a minute. All those people who couldn't afford to rent from me without the government's help were beating at my door, looking for housing at government-subsidized prices.

Availability of tenants leads to freedom of choice. The more tenants who were available, the more selective I could afford to be. To me, this meant Uncle Sam was helping me to upgrade my properties. If I had to rely on the private housing market to get tenants, the supply would have been severely limited. I would have had two basic choices: either be less selective about the tenants I picked or lower my rents.

Either way, I would have made less money than I made by working with the government. Some of my best tenants were the ones with the lowest incomes. Little old ladies and gentlemen who had worked hard all their lives, but had little or nothing to show for it. Getting good tenants attracted other good tenants, and that benefited me in a number of ways: Good tenants mean less maintenance and repairs. They don't tear up the apartments and then call the landlord every time the faucet starts leaking. They don't start arguments and fights.

Good management means stability. Most important, good tenants mean stability and that means you don't get a lot of vacancies. You attract tenants who move in and stay and begin to think of the property as their home. They take care of the property and they pay their rent on time. They don't cause trouble or do anything to make their home a less desirable place in which to live. The more desirable a building is to live in, the more desirable it is to own. This increases the value.

Stability means higher income and greater profits. Good, stable tenants also mean higher income from the property, because people will

139

pay more to live in a good, stable building. Transients tend to attract other transients and drive away the stable, long-term tenants who are the ones you really want to deal with. They give a building the wrong type of atmosphere.

When tenants are transient and no one knows his neighbors, vandalism and crime increase. No one feels any real sense of responsibility to the property or to others. If someone goes out for a while, or goes away for a few days or weeks, their neighbors won't know or care enough to watch their apartment while they're out.

STABLE TENANTS AND MINIMAL PROBLEMS

My government-subsidized tenants weren't like that. They tended to be long-term and responsible. There was a long waiting list to get into the subsidized housing program, which meant that most of my government-subsidized tenants were long-time residents of the area. They were not drifters or short-term renters. They were people who stayed put as long as they were treated right.

What value do you put on peace of mind? This can't be measured in dollars and cents alone. There is also the psychological effect, the peace of mind that comes from owning property that is running smoothly. What scares most people away from investing in real estate? Management. They are afraid of dealing with tenants and most of them have good reason to be scared. Tenants can easily be the biggest problem you will ever have as a landlord. But the government can help you eliminate that problem.

Increased income doesn't hurt either. Peace of mind is nice. In fact, it's wonderful. But don't ever underestimate the value of increased income. First, increased income can help give you peace of mind. There's nothing nicer than knowing that you've got the bills paid each month and still have a bit left over. That is one of the most peaceful feelings I know.

There are things that periodically go wrong when you own property, and it's definitely nice to know you've got the income to get them corrected when necessary. If you have to start dipping into your own pocket for money for repairs and maintenance, then the idea of owning investment real estate quickly loses its appeal. The idea is for your property to support you within a short period of time after you begin investing. If you have to support the property instead, something is wrong. After all, how long would you walk around dragging your car behind you if it stopped working? Not very long, right? So why drag a property along behind you when it's not running right? That's what you're doing when you support a property that has a negative cash flow.

PAINLESS RENT RAISES

Government subsidies end negative cash flow. Since the government was subsidizing their rents, my tenants could afford to pay more. This doesn't mean I had a license to steal and could raise the rents as high as I wanted. They were strictly regulated by the government and I was allowed to charge only what the government was willing to pay.

This was still higher than the going rents on the open market, in many cases. My tenants were happy to pay it, since only a small portion of it was coming out of their pockets and because they knew they were getting better housing that way.

Higher rents mean higher property values. People who buy income property are looking for income. The more the better. It's a very simple formula. Most property is evaluated on the basis of the gross yearly income. (My graduates learn to evaluate property on the basis of net income, after expenses, but the basic principle is the same: When you increase the income, you increase the value.)

Investors like to see that extra income coming in each month. They also like the idea that the rents are subsidized. They know the government is not about to skip town or go out of business, so they know they will get their rents each and every month. This increases the value of the property too. What does it prove to have a good income in theory, if you never actually collect it? This is a definite fear that many potential buyers have and for good reason. Many sellers pump up the income just before they sell their properties and by doing this, they create problems for the buyer.

Government-guaranteed subsidies helps sell properties for top dollar. In this case, prospective buyers would know that the government has guaranteed the rents, and possibly more important, the government has guaranteed that the rents wouldn't be a burden on the tenants. They pay a certain fixed percentage of their incomes, and the government takes care of the rest. Accordingly, good tenants are never forced to move because they can no longer afford to pay the rent.

SIT BACK AND ENJOY IT

You don't have to fight city hall when you can work with it instead and make lots of money. Sure, there may be lots of things that the government does wrong, but why focus on it? Focus instead on some of the good things the government does and particularly the good things these government programs can do for you to help you get started in your investing career. For example, our next chapter will show you how you can buy government-owned real estate for pennies on the dollar.

KEY POINTS TO REMEMBER

1. Government repos are available to anyone who qualifies.
2. Some government repos come with built-in financing. Others are sold on a strictly all-cash basis.
3. In certain target areas you can get purchase and rehab loans at special low interest.
4. Guaranteed rents make properties saleable.
5. The government is anxious to unload these properties, but only if you can prove that you are a reliable buyer.
6. Section 8 tenants tend to be more stable.
7. Stable tenants tend to attract other stable tenants.
8. Subsidized tenants can afford to pay more rent.
9. The government sets goals and quotas based on local needs.

CHAPTER TEN

GOVERNMENT-OWNED REAL ESTATE FOR PENNIES ON THE DOLLAR

FORECLOSURES AND SEIZED PROPERTIES

Foreclosures can be one of the best opportunities around, because you are dealing with people who are in no position to bargain. Once a property goes into foreclosure, it means the owner has given up. He can't meet his responsibilities and has stopped trying. Any equity he has built up is as good as gone. Any benefits he expected to get when he sold the property are forfeited. Real estate is often called the most forgiving investment, and it is, but there are also limits. An owner usually has several chances to save himself before foreclosure. But once the foreclosure sale is set up, that is it. This is the grim side of foreclosure.

People lose their properties and all their hope and hard work and dreams evaporate overnight. It is well deserved in some cases. In other cases, the people involved are unfortunate victims of circumstances. In any event, the law of nature says that for every action there is an equal and opposite reaction. This works in real estate as well—at least as far as foreclosures are concerned. For every person who loses out in a foreclosure, there is someone else who wins. This section is about how you can become one of those winners.

WHAT IS A FORECLOSURE?

First of all, let's start off by talking about what a foreclosure is and go through the whole foreclosure process from the start. This way, you can get a clear picture of exactly what happens, in what sequence, and how you can make money on it. First of all, foreclosure is the process whereby a lender takes a property away from a borrower who has violated the loan agreement between them. It is a legal proceeding that may or may not require the lender to go to court and appear before a judge, depending on whether the loan is secured by a mortgage or a trust deed. It can take anywhere from four months to a year or more from start to finish.

Not every loan can lead to a foreclosure if the borrower defaults. The loan must be secured by real estate in the first place, in order for the lender to foreclose. There are three main ways of securing a loan with real estate: A mortgage, a trust deed, or a land contract of sale. The contract of sale is not used with government loans (except in some cases when foreclosed properties are resold on contracts), so we will skip over that and concentrate on mortgages and trust deeds.

MORTGAGES

Mortgages are the most common way to secure real estate loans, whether those loans are government-insured or not. They are allowed in every state, although they are not used very frequently in states that allow trust deeds. A mortgage is basically a document by which someone pledges a piece of property as security for a loan.

If the buyer violates the loan agreement, the lender can go to court and seek a court order allowing him to seize the property. The borrower retains title to the property, but the mortgage is recorded as a lien against the property, and he can't sell the property without paying off that lien. If he violates the loan agreement, the first step for the lender is to file a Notice of Default. This is the official notice that the borrower is in violation of the loan agreement and the lender intends to file a foreclosure action.

Generally, this means that the borrower has not been making his payments, but it could also involve other causes, such as a failure by the borrower to pay the insurance premiums or taxes as required by the loan agreement. With government-insured loans, the taxes and insurance are usually included in the payment, so this won't normally apply. If the property is being foreclosed on, it is usually because the borrower didn't make the payments or lied on his loan application. Once the lender files a Notice of Default, he goes to court and asks for a hearing on his petition to foreclose on the property.

REQUEST FOR A MORATORIUM

With government-insured loans, the lender can also go to the insuring agency—HUD/FHA, the Veterans Administration, or the Farmers Home Administration—and ask the agency to take over the loan. The borrower can also ask the government to take over the loan in some cases. For example, with HUD/FHA Homebuyer Loans, borrowers can ask for a moratorium or adjustment of their payments if they are having financial difficulties. They will not automatically get it. They will have to demonstrate legitimate need, first of all. But that possibility is always open. If they do not get a moratorium or adjustment of their payments, the borrowers still have up to a year or more to hold on to their property and have the payments straightened out. This is how long it normally takes for a foreclosure hearing and a final order giving the lender the right to seize the property.

Once the property is seized, it is put up for sale at auction and sold to the highest bidder. The borrower's equity is at the mercy of the bidders. If the price gets bid up high enough, he may still get something out of the property. If not, he gets nothing.

HARRY IS IN TROUBLE

For example, let's say Hapless Harry bought a house five years ago for $50,000 and he took out a $45,000 FHA loan at 9.5%. Today, the house is worth $75,000 and the loan is paid down to $43,290. Or it would be if Harry had not fallen behind in his payments. He lost his job and he

147

owes four months' worth of payments for a total of more than $1,900, including taxes and insurance, plus another $100 in late charges. The lender files for foreclosure and by the time the house actually comes up for auction, Harry owes over $6,000 plus foreclosure charges.

The lender adds all this to the $43,290 that Harry owes on the principal of the loan and comes up with a figure of $50,000. This will be the minimum bid at the foreclosure sale. Anything over $50,000 will go to Hapless Harry. The first $50,000 will go to the lender.

At first sight, it might seem that Harry is in a good position to collect some money. And he might be if he were selling the house himself. After all, the house is worth $75,000. But even with all of his problems, he only owed the lender $50,000. The only problem is that he is not selling the house himself. The lender or FHA is selling the house. Either way, they cannot get more than $50,000 out of it and they do not have to accept any bids of less than $50,000. They can just take the property and keep it if no acceptable bids come in. Then they can sell it and give Hapless Harry nothing, no matter how much the house sells for.

Of course, the lender has an obligation to try to get the highest possible price for the house. It has to be advertised and the public must be given every chance to bid on it. But the lender and the FHA are under no obligation to knock themselves out to see that Hapless Harry gets to salvage some of his equity. They don't have to advertise extensively or spend any real money on advertising. Simple flyers and ads in legal newspapers are sufficient.

FORECLOSURE SALES ARE NOT FOR EVERYONE

They don't have to offer any special terms or interest rates or anything like that. In fact, in many states, foreclosure sales are conducted on a strictly cash basis. Needless to say, this discourages a lot of would-be buyers. Foreclosure sales are not for everyone, and those who do bid at foreclosure sales are usually experienced investors who do not expect to pay anywhere near the market value.

Foreclosure sales are for bargain hunters. They are the place to pick up cast-off properties which can be purchased for far less than they are worth. If Hapless Harry's house is worth $75,000 on the open market, it will probably sell for $50,000 to $60,000 at the foreclosure sale. Let's say Harry is finally lucky. His house sells for $60,000 at the foreclosure sale. This means that he will get $10,000 out of the sale. He has lost $15,000 in equity by not selling the house himself.

Actually, he may have lost even more than that, because he would not have had the foreclosure charges if he had sold it himself. But things could be worse. If the house had brought bids of under $50,000, Harry would have gotten nothing. Harry also has a chance to get the property back. Depending on where he lives, he may have up to two years after the foreclosure sale to redeem the property and buy it back. Naturally, this tends to discourage buyers and help keep the price down at foreclosure auctions, so it is a mixed blessing. But it means Harry still has a chance.

DEEDS OF TRUST

If Harry lives in a state where deeds of trust are legal, he may not even have that chance. Trust deeds allow the lender to bypass the courts if the borrower defaults on the loan agreement. In fact, until the loan is paid off, the borrower does not even hold the title to his own property. Title is held by a theoretically neutral third party known as the trustee.

I say theoretically neutral, because the trustee is actually an employee of the lender. If the borrower defaults on the loan, the lender contacts the trustee and it is the trustee who files the Notice of Default and begins the foreclosure proceeding. The trustee does not have to go to court or consult with a judge to do this. There are definite rules to govern his conduct, but he is allowed to initiate and follow through on the entire foreclosure process on his own.

THE BORROWER CAN REDEEM THE LOAN

Once the trustee has filed the Notice of Default, there is a three-month waiting period known as the default period. During this time, the borrower can redeem the loan simply by making up any back payments and paying the default charges. The lender can refuse to accept partial payment but must accept full payment if it is offered and stop the foreclosure action. Once the default period is over, the trustee must publish a Notice of Sale. The sale cannot be held for at least three weeks from the date the notice is published. It is final. The borrower has no right of redemption. When the sale is over, he cannot get the property back.

On the other hand, the lender cannot get a deficiency judgment if the foreclosure sale brings in less than $50,000. All he can do is take over the property—or ask the government to take over the property and repay the loan for the borrower. Once that happens, whichever government agency guaranteed the loan will take over the property and resell it. Now it is no longer a foreclosure sale and so foreclosure sale rules don't apply.

BARGAIN PROPERTIES

The agency involved—FHA/HUD, VA, or FmHA—sets the rules. You can write to all of these agencies, or call or visit your local office, and get lists of their repossessed properties for sale. The lists will tell you what the rules are for bidding on these properties, how much down payment is required, what financing is available, etc. It will vary, depending on the property and the area, and go according to what the local office of the agency involved feels it can get for the property.

You can find bargain properties from these repossessed property lists, you can get them at the original foreclosure sales, or you can buy them directly from the owners before the foreclosure sales. Therefore, you have at least three different ways to make money.

BUYING DISTRESS PROPERTIES FROM THE OWNER

Let's start at the beginning and assume that you are going to talk to property-owners who are in trouble. In order to do this you must first know how to locate and identify them. Then you have to learn to convince them that dealing with you is the best alternative they have and that you will help them solve their problems, not compound them. This should not be quite as difficult as it sounds.

Remember, most of these people are confused and afraid. They are not really in control of their situation. If they were, their properties would not be on the verge of foreclosure. They are people who are used to being passive, to leaving their fate in the hands of others. You can be one of those other people and be well paid for it. You don't have to be a vulture, stealing properties from helpless people. You can save people's credit ratings, help them to salvage at least some of the equity in their homes, and still buy those homes for a lot less than market value.

151

ADVERTISING

As a starter, join organizations where you meet people and hear things. Groups like the Lions, the Elks, veterans' organizations, etc. Cultivate hairdressers, milkmen, newspaper boys, shopkeepers, anyone who knows the area and its people (who is moving, who is getting divorced, who lost his job, etc.).

Let all of these people know that you buy real estate and pay referral fees for good deals that people tell you about. Have cards printed up, advertising that you buy real estate. Present them whenever you have the opportunity. If this doesn't bring responses as fast as you would like, consider being a little more aggressive. Maybe you really need to advertise.

Call a couple of local newspapers, the ones that carry all the real estate ads, and find out what it would cost to run one of your own. Chances are, it won't be nearly as much as you think, especially since you probably need to run it only on Sundays. The ad doesn't have to be elaborate. In fact, the simpler you keep it, the better off you will be. You don't want to give anyone the idea that you are a slick professional investor. You are just a person trying to get ahead by buying a little bit of real estate for yourself. If you can help solve other people's problems by taking properties they can't handle, all the better. Something like this: "I buy real estate. Any condition. Cash. Fast closing." Or "I buy real estate if you will sell with no money down." Or even "I buy property. Talk to me today and close escrow tomorrow." Ads like this are short and to the point. They tell people what they need to know and they don't cost very much to run. One good response will pay for the ad for a whole year or more.

LOOK FOR KEY PHRASES

You should also keep your eyes open for other people's ads. Many property-owners facing the loss of their properties try to sell the properties themselves before they lose everything. Their ads are usually fairly easy to spot if you know what to look for. There are certain key phrases that are easy to spot: Seller Anxious; Seller Flexible; Creative Financing; Fast Close Desired; All Reasonable Offers Considered; Price Reduced; Name Your Own Terms; and on and on. . . .

Of course, you must be careful; not all sellers who use these phrases are sincere. Many of them are not in any trouble at all, and in such cases they are just using those phrases deliberately to lure unsuspecting buyers who will think they are getting a deal when they really are not. You have to learn to wade through these people and spot them when you talk to them on the phone so you do not waste valuable time.

QUALIFYING SELLERS ON THE PHONE

Learning to qualify sellers on the phone is an art of its own. You want to establish right away that you are the one who is controlling the situation. You are interested in buying property, but you are not necessarily interested in buying his property. He has to convince you it is worth your while to buy his property. How hard he works at this over the phone will tell you how sincere the seller is and how anxious he really is to sell his property.

Naturally, you want to know where the property is located. Even if the address is listed in the ad and you are familiar with it, ask questions. You want to see how much the seller will tell you and how hard he will try to sell you the property. Does he just give you the information you ask for or does he go on at length telling you all the good things about the property and the neighborhood? Does he act as though it is all the same to him, whether you do or don't come over to look at the house? Does he act as though he has been swamped with calls and is starting to get bored with the whole thing?

If so, he is not the seller you want to deal with. If he is not excited about trying to sell you the property, how can you get excited about trying to buy it? You have to conserve your time and energy. There are lots of properties out there and you have time to see only a few of them. If the sellers want you to come and look at their property, they have to convince you it will be worth your while. Don't be afraid to make them work. Put them through their paces.

ASK QUESTIONS

Have a complete list of questions ready and don't be afraid to ask them all:

> What is the financing?
> How long does the current loan have to run?
> How much down payment does the seller need or want?
> What is he going to do with the money?
> Has he thought about what he will do if he doesn't get it?
> What will he do if he can't sell the property?
> Has he thought about it?
> What is the lowest price the seller will accept?
> Will he take no money down?
> How much paper will he carry?

What interest rate does he expect to charge?

How did he arrive at that interest rate?

How did he arrive at the asking price?

Has the property been on the market for very long?

How long?

Has the seller had any offers?

How many?

How come he didn't accept them?

Has he thought about what will happen if the property doesn't sell soon?

What are the schools like?

The transportation?

What is the area like?

Who are the neighbors and what do they do?

Is it a high-crime area?

What are the property taxes like?

The utility bills?

Asking questions like this will tell you how prepared the seller is. Does he have all the answers right at hand, or does he keep telling you he is not sure? You can find out a lot about the sellers you deal with even before you ever meet them in person and that can be a powerful aid in negotiations. The more you know about a person, the easier it is to deal with him.

MAKING THE INITIAL VISIT

When a seller and a property meet your initial qualifications over the telephone, set up an appointment to see the property in person. But first make sure the appointment is at your convenience and not the seller's. He has all the time in the world, as far as you are concerned. After all, he is the one with a property to sell. Your time is valuable. You have a lot of other things to do besides looking at his property.

ESTABLISH CONTROL

Whatever time the seller suggests is no good. You are sorry, but you have a couple of other properties to look at at that time, way over on the other side of town. However, you will be over on the seller's side of town at another time that would be more convenient for you. "How about then?"

Mention that it must be extremely nervewracking to be in their position, facing the loss of their home. You don't want to overdo this, because it will probably backfire and make them hostile.

But if you can sound sympathetic, as though you really feel sorry for them, you might be able to soften them up and make friends. You don't want to sound too friendly at this point, however. You want to keep your distance from the sellers and the property. You are not ready to deal yet unless the sellers are really anxious. You are still just feeling them out at this point. Walk around the house, mutter to yourself, take notes. Act as if you keep finding things you don't like. If a seller asks if anything is wrong, smile and say no. Then, go on muttering and taking notes and shaking your head and doing anything else you can think of to make the sellers uncomfortable and to convince them that you don't like the house but are just too polite to say so. Be polite and friendly.

DON'T OVER-REACT

You will not gain anything by being rude. The whole idea is to be relatively enthusiastic when you walk in and then to gradually lose that enthusiasm as you walk around the house. You are doing your best to cover it up, so how can the seller be mad? But it is bound to make him uncomfortable and insecure. Ideally, it will just reinforce all of his fears about what is wrong with the house. Eventually, he may even open up and start confessing to you about all that is wrong and then try to convince you to buy the house anyway. This may sound far-fetched, but it happens all the time.

Often, your very best source of information about the property will be the owner himself. Sure, some owners are dishonest and will deliberately try to cover up any problems with the property. But most property-owners are honest and they will tell you everything, especially if they get nervous and insecure. Don't over-react to anything the seller does tell you, but make it clear that it does lower the value of the property. That is the whole point of the initial inspection: You just want the seller to know that the property is not worth what he thinks or hopes it is worth.

MORE NEGOTIATING TACTICS

You want to prepare him for selling to you on your terms, not his. The bedrooms are nice, but small. The living room, dining room, kitchen, etc., are not quite what you had in mind.

None of these are insurmountable problems—you could conceivably be talked into buying the house anyway—but they are problems. Now, what does the seller intend to do about them? Is he going to take the chance that you will slip through his fingers? Or is he going to make sure that you don't slip away by doing whatever must be done to accommodate you? If he lets you get out the door, don't worry about it. There are plenty of other sellers out there who may be a bit more eager to do business. You might just say that you want to think about the house and you will call him if you decide you are interested.

Is He Really Serious About Selling?

Or you might stop in the doorway, look the seller in the eye, and say something like: "Would you be able to give me an immediate answer if I made you an offer right now? What would you really take? Right now. No more waiting and no more fooling around. . . ." Whichever approach you take, stay friendly and cheerful. If he is really serious about selling before he is foreclosed on, he will never let you get out the door that easily anyway.

In any case, keep in mind—and try to keep it in the seller's mind—that you are possibly his last hope. He is going to lose his property unless someone buys it soon. If he realizes the full implications of this, he will stop you right there and try to work out some sort of deal. He won't want you to walk out the door, not without making one last effort to interest you in the house. If he doesn't make an effort to stop you, just write your name and phone number on a piece of paper and give it to him.

MAKE IT LOOK CASUAL

Don't use a business card, because that looks too slick and professional. Just make it look casual and tell him to call you if he changes his mind and decides he is really anxious to sell. Then, leave. Don't call him again. Wait for him to call you. If he does, fine. If he doesn't, then find another property. Chances are he will call you eventually, since time is on your side. The longer the clock keeps ticking away, the closer he gets to foreclosure. The main thing you want is that low-interest loan. That is what makes the property appealing. You want to take over the loan at the original interest rate, with as little cash down as possible.

If the seller wants something for his equity and does not just want to give up and walk away from the property, that is understandable. Offer him a note. He will get something out of his property, but you will not have to strain yourself to get into it.

Even if you have to give the seller a little cash for his equity, that is all right, as long as you don't give him too much. You can't expect to get every property for just the amount of the outstanding loan. That would be nice, but unfortunately it is not too realistic, so you just take the best deals you can get. If nothing you find suits you, it is on to the next step.

Buying Government-Financed Properties at the Foreclosure Sale

Foreclosure sales are easy to find. They have to be advertised. The idea is to attract the largest possible number of bidders to get the price up as high as possible, so all the creditors will get their money and the former owner might even get something out of it.

All you have to do is get any legal newspaper and the notices of impending foreclosure sales will be listed, including information about the time and place for the sale. The thing that is usually not listed in the foreclosure notices is the position that the foreclosed loan is in (i.e., first, second, third, etc.). This is important information. It is not always easy to get.

Some lenders will give you the information with no trouble. Others will either refuse to cooperate or may even lie to you, telling you that a third is a second, or a first, etc. It is extremely important to find out what position the loan is really in. Otherwise, you won't know what you are bidding on. You may not be getting free and clear title to the property. You may be bidding just for the right to take the property subject to the senior loans, and that is quite different.

Be Sure You Know What You're Bidding On

For example, let's say you see a foreclosure sale advertised in a legal paper and it seems like something you would be interested in. The foreclosed loan is for $35,000 and you know that properties in the area are worth at least $60,000 to $65,000. It appears there should be a good bit of equity there. So you go to the foreclosure sale and are surprised to find that you are the only one there.

You thought you might have to go as high as $40,000. Instead, you get the property for the minimum bid. You expect to make $20,000 on the transaction, even after expenses. What a sweet deal.

What a rude awakening when you find out that you have taken the property subject to a first loan of $30,000. No wonder the ex-owner walked away and let the property go into foreclosure. No wonder he kept up the payments on the first loan and let the second foreclose. The first loan is insured by FHA. The second loan is private. He didn't want to get in trouble with the government for overcranking the property (borrowing more than the true value of the property and defrauding the lender).

Is There Any Equity in the Property?

This sort of unfortunate incident happens to people every day. How can you avoid it? You have to do a careful check of the property records and find out the amounts of any loans filed as liens against the property, as well as the dates when they were recorded. This is the only way to find out which loan is in what position. Without such information, you never know if there is really any equity in the property at all. For example, you go to the county records and find out that there are two loans against the property: The $30,000 loan was recorded on May 1, 1975. The $35,000 loan was not recorded until December 20, 1976. That tells you the first loan is the one for $30,000, because it was recorded first.

Even if the borrower took out the $35,000 loan first, it wouldn't matter. The loan in the first position in case of a foreclosure is the loan that was recorded first. The only exception to this rule is when a subordination agreement has been filed. This means that the holder of the note that would normally be in first, second, third position, etc., has agreed to subordinate his loan to other loans put on the property at a later time.

CHECK THE RECORDS CAREFULLY

This would have to be in the county records along with the deed and all the various loans against the property. If it is not recorded, it has no legal standing. If the first or second loan is government-insured or subsidized, it will not be subordinated to any other loans in the future.

But there could be other previously recorded loans which were subordinated to the new government-insured or subsidized financing. So check all the records carefully. You may want to consider seriously the idea of leaving it to the professionals. If you live in an area where there are title and escrow companies, let them do the title search for you.

Even though you can't get title insurance very easily on foreclosure properties, particularly in mortgage states with long right-of-redemption periods, you can have the title researched by the experts. It is well worth the fee to have peace of mind.

One of the major title companies likes to advertise that Abraham Lincoln once lost his house because of a bad title and asks if you want to take that risk. It is definitely a risk that one should try to minimize. If there are no title companies in your area, go to a lawyer. In most states, foreclosure sales are all cash, final sales. In some states, you can put up a deposit and take thirty days to come up with the balance, but they are still not for amateurs because mistakes can be costly.

BUYING POST-FORECLOSURE BARGAINS FROM THE GOVERNMENT

If all this sounds too intimidating, you can always wait until after the foreclosure sale and try to pick up properties after various government agencies have taken them over. These are the properties that did not sell at the foreclosure auctions.

For example, let's say a property had a $50,000 FHA loan against it and $3,000 worth of back payments, late charges, etc., to be made up. This means the minimum bid at the foreclosure sale is going to be $53,000. If no one bids at least that much, FHA buys the property for $53,000 and then resells it.

Once the foreclosure sale is over and FHA takes over the property, the foreclosure laws no longer apply, and the sale is conducted according to FHA rules (or VA or FmHA or whatever agency has taken over the property). Whatever the property sells for, the government gets all the money. The ex-owner gets nothing. Any equity he had is lost.

Often, the government will offer financing on these foreclosed properties which normally sell for well below market value. To find out about them, contact your local HUD/FHA, VA, or FmHA office or write to the main offices in Washington and get on a mailing list, so you will receive regular information about these properties.

PROPERTIES SEIZED FROM TAX DELINQUENTS AND CRIMINALS

Besides properties that have been foreclosed on, the government also has properties that have been seized for one reason or another. The IRS has long had the power to seize the property of those who owed back taxes. Law enforcement agencies such as the FBI and the Drug Enforcement Agency (DEA) are now also empowered to seize the property of convicted criminals who accumulated their wealth illegally.

The IRS is, of course, familiar with money and dealing with seized properties. Other branches of the Treasury and Justice departments are not set up for this sort of activity. It is only recently that they have been ordered to participate in seizing and selling properties. In many cases, they are anxious to be rid of the properties and get them off their hands. Since the properties didn't cost the government anything, they are not always concerned about getting top dollar for them. This can mean bargains for you. However, like foreclosure sales, these sales are usually all cash, with no returns or refunds.

To bid on these properties, contact the agency involved, either in Washington, D.C., or at your local office, and get on their mailing list. Accordingly, you will receive information on a regular basis concerning seized properties that are coming up for sale, just like government-owned foreclosure properties.

HUD REPOSSESSED PROJECTS

Then, there are the big projects. Sometimes, they go under too. So HUD or FmHA has to find someone new to take over these projects. You have to apply to HUD or FmHA and prove you are qualified and competent to do the job. This can be another source of lucrative opportunities.

KEY POINTS TO REMEMBER

1. Government-insured loans can be secured by either a mortgage or a trust deed, depending on which state the property is located in.
2. Mortgage foreclosures are known as judicial foreclosures, because the lender has to go to court and get permission from a judge in order to foreclose on the borrower's property.
3. Trust deed foreclosures are known as non-judicial foreclosures, because the trustee handles all the details, without having to go to court.
4. Mortgage foreclosures can take up to a year or more.
5. Trust deed foreclosures take about four months.
6. The ex-property-owner may have a right of redemption up to two years or more after the foreclosure sale.
7. There is no right of redemption with a trust deed foreclosure.
8. Notices of Default and Notices of Sale must be published in newspapers of general circulation (generally legal newspapers).
9. Foreclosure sales are normally "as is," with no contingencies, no guarantees, and no returns.
10. If no acceptable bids are received at the foreclosure sale, the lender or the government usually takes over the property.
11. After the foreclosure sale, each agency sets its own rules for sales of seized properties.
12. Besides foreclosures, the government also has properties seized by the IRS and the Justice and Treasury departments.

CHAPTER ELEVEN

GET BACK ALL THE TAXES YOU PAID IN THE LAST THREE YEARS

There are many ways to take advantage of Uncle Sam's generosity even if you don't want to borrow any money. The easiest way to do this is through the use of special tax write-offs that can leave you with more money to spend and less to give away to the government. Everyone knows real estate is one of the best tax shelters available. This is one of the main reasons why many people invest in real estate. There are the interest deductions, the write-offs for depreciation, and all the business expenses you can write off, such as an office in your home, simply because you are in the business of buying and owning real estate.

All of these write-offs exist. They are real and they are very useful. They can cut your tax bill way down. But, as with most things that everyone knows about, this is not the whole story. Not by a long shot. There are other tax write-offs for certain specific real estate investments that most people are not even aware of.

These special tax incentives can turn a mediocre investment—or even an outright loser—into a profitable money maker. However, this is not really surprising if you understand the tax laws, because that is exactly what they are supposed to do. Most people do not understand this. If they did, we would not have all the foolish talk and periodic rumors of a new, more equitable flat-rate tax system.

WHAT THE TAX SYSTEM IS DESIGNED TO DO

The tax system is set up to do more than just collect money. It is designed to stimulate the economy and encourage people to invest their money the way the government wants them to. This is why we will never have a flat-rate tax system. Taxes are not supposed to be equitable. That would not serve the government's purposes very well. The tax laws are deliberately set up to "reward" those who know how to play the game and "punish" those who don't. The more you understand, the less you pay. This is what keeps our economy going.

Those of us who don't want to pay taxes and don't want to go to jail for evading them, either, learn to do what the government wants us to do—like invest our money in real estate—and the money we save creates jobs and gives people rental housing to live in when they cannot afford to buy a house.

In the long run, the country benefits more from this than it would from getting the extra tax money. This is why investing in real estate provides tax shelter and it is also why certain types of real estate investments produce even more tax write-offs.

Rehabbing Makes Sense

The nice part about it is that doing what the government wants you to do is not always such a bad idea anyway. Many of the investments the government wants to encourage make good sense even without special tax breaks. Taking rehabbing older properties as an example. Rehabbing makes sense with or without government tax breaks.

As a lot of you probably know, I am very partial to rehabbing myself, because I have made a lot of money with it. It's what got me started in real estate. One of the cornerstones of the Lowry philosophy has always been to find a run-down property, fix it up, and make money on it. Today this idea makes even more sense as inner-cities are being revitalized all over the country and older properties are finding new life, while their owners find new profits they had long ago given up on.

The economics of the eighties make rehabbing a winner. Recent research has determined that it costs ten times as much, on average, to construct a new building as it would to rehab an existing one. But will a new building bring in ten times the income? Not very likely. When you add in the special government tax credits you can get for certain types of rehab projects, all you are doing is adding the gravy to an already fine meal. And this is just what the government has done.

So now we are going to talk about those tax credits and how you can cash in on them and get some of that gravy—and the "meat and potatoes" to go with it.

THE 15% REHABILITATION TAX CREDIT

We are starting with this one because it is the smallest of the rehabilitation tax credits offered and the easiest one to qualify for. From here, we go on to even bigger and better things, but this is a fun place to start. After all, who can't use a nice dollar-for-dollar write-off against any taxes you might owe? All you have to do to earn it is to buy a building at least thirty years old and renovate it.

It sounds simple, doesn't it? That's because it is. No one is trying to make it hard for you. The government wants to make it easy for you to qualify for this one. That's what it's all about. Of course, there are a couple of minor catches, but nothing that should prevent you from making lots of money.

First, the tax credit only applies to non-residential properties. You can't get it by buying and renovating houses or apartment buildings, unless—and this is an important point that many people, even experienced tax advisors, are confused about—the property is to be used for low-income housing and has been certified by HUD as an approved project. Otherwise, it has to be storefronts, or office space, or industrial and warehouse space, or any type of property that is used to produce income for the owner(s) but is not residential.

Think about the area where you live. Do you really think you would have too hard a time finding such properties that could use some renovation work done to them? Chances are, you will find at least a few.

The second catch is that you must spend at least as much on the renovation as you did in buying the property in the first place. If you buy a property for $100,000, you have to spend at least $100,000 renovating it in order to qualify for the tax credit. The government is paying people to fix up old buildings and restore them to life, not just buy them and let them sit the way they are or slap on a coat of paint and do a few minor repairs. They expect you to do some serious work.

169

The third catch is that half the tax credit gets deducted from the depreciable basis of the property. This cuts down the amount of depreciation available to you and, therefore, takes away some of the ongoing tax write-off you would normally get in later years. This means you save more than you normally would the first year. But then you get to write off slightly less than you would in the remaining years you hold the building.

HOLD THE BUILDING AT LEAST FIVE YEARS

There is a simple solution to that, you say? Just buy the building, renovate it, take the tax credit, and then sell the place. That way you won't have to worry about getting less than the normal amount of depreciation in later years. It's an excellent idea. The only problem is, it won't work!

Here is the final catch: In order to get the full 15% tax credit, you have to hold the building for at least five years. You get a 3% credit for every year you hold it, up to the maximum. You can take the full 15% tax credit all in the first year, but if you sell the building before five years have gone by, you have to repay 20% of the tax credit for each year that you won't own the property anymore.

In other words, if you only hold the property for three years, you would only be entitled to 60% of the total tax credit, or 9% of the cost of the renovation work. (In this case, $9,000 or 9% of the $100,000 you spent on renovations.)

If you had already taken the full credit the first year, you would owe the IRS the difference. Does all of this sound confusing? It's actually quite simple, once you understand it, so let's run through a typical example. Okay. Here we go.

First, let's assume you have a tax problem, or at least owe some taxes, and this is one reason why you specifically decided to buy a property to qualify for special tax treatment. After all your deductions have been figured, you still owe the IRS $25,000 for the year, and you want to cut that down as far as possible—to zero, if you can.

So your tax advisor told you about this special program and you decided to try it. You have all the work done and you want to figure out how much you have saved. The 15% tax credit comes off your tax bill, dollar for dollar.

You spent $100,000 on the renovations, so you get to deduct $15,000 from your tax bill. This means you only owe $10,000, instead of $25,000. That is the difference between a tax credit and a tax write-off. The write-off (for example, depreciation) is deducted from your taxable income, reducing the amount of income on which you must pay taxes. The tax credit is a direct dollar-for-dollar write-off against any taxes you owe after you have figured in all of the deductions. This is what makes it so valuable.

Now, some of you may be wondering why you can take a credit of only $100,000. After all, you spent $100,000 buying the building and another $100,000 fixing it up. That totals $200,000. Unfortunately, you can take the tax credit only for the cost of the actual renovations. You cannot include the purchase price of the property. That must be depreciated instead.

Depreciation Benefits

So that is why you get only a $15,000 tax credit in this case. But the tax credit is not the end of your tax benefits. You still get to take depreciation on the cost of the building itself. Since you paid $100,000 for the whole property, we will arbitrarily assign a value of $20,000 to the land underneath the building. This is a nice, safe, conservative figure, 20%

of the total purchase price, and we shouldn't get any trouble from the IRS. (Of course, in real life, you may want to be more aggressive and allocate a smaller portion of the purchase price to the nondepreciable land.) It leaves you with a depreciable basis of $80,000 for the building itself. Now you have to deduct half of the $15,000 tax credit ($7,500) from this amount and you are left with a new basis for depreciation of $72,500 ($80,000 minus $7,500). This is the value that you can actually use for depreciating the property for tax purposes.

So now that you know what your depreciable basis is, you start to figure out how much you will actually save on depreciation. You divide $72,500 by 18 years under the new 1984 tax law and you come up with $4,027 worth of depreciation each year for the next 18 years. Since you are in the 50% tax bracket, this saves you a little over $2,000 a year beyond what you saved on tax credits. That is really not a bad deal if you think about it. If you had two projects like that in one year, you would not have to pay any taxes at all.

But that's not all Uncle Sam has in store for you. Our next program is almost exactly the same as this one, with one little twist: It's even better.

THE 20% REHABILITATION TAX CREDIT

What do you have to do to get a 20% Rehabilitation Tax Credit instead of a 15% tax credit? It's simple. Just buy an older building. Instead of getting one that is at least 30 years old, make sure it is at least 40 years old. It is as simple as that. All the other rules of the game are the same. The rehab work must cost at least as much as the building itself, you have to deduct half the amount of the tax credit from the depreciable basis of the building, and you can only use standard, 18-year straight-line depreciation. (The only difference is that the building must be ten years older in order to qualify for the extra 5% tax credit for rehabbing it.)

So now let's run through some numbers again and see how that extra tax credit can make a difference on your taxes. Let's stick with the $100,000 purchase price and $100,000 in rehab costs. This time you get to take a tax credit of $20,000, so your remaining tax bill is cut down to only $5,000 (instead of $25,000) even before you take any depreciation write-off. Half of the tax credit is $10,000 and that's how much you have to subtract from your depreciable basis, so you are left with $70,-000 worth of depreciable improvements for tax purposes.

You divide $70,000 by 18 years and you get $3,888. This is how much you get to deduct from your taxable income for the year. Since you are in the 50% tax bracket, this reduces your remaining tax bill by half of that amount ($1,944). You then subtract this amount from the $5,000 you still owe the IRS and you come up with a final tax bill of $3,056. That's not as good as paying nothing, but it sure is a lot better than paying the $25,000 you originally owed.

Now we are going to take the whole process one step further. Earlier, I mentioned that if you bought two of these properties in one year, you would not have to pay any taxes at all. So we are going to assume that you did buy and renovate two of these projects in the same year and see exactly how it would work out for you.

We are going to assume that you start off with the same $25,000 tax obligation after all of your other deductions. We are also going to assume that you bought and renovated two buildings, one 35 years old and the other 40 years old. Just to keep everything simple, we are going to assume that you also spent $100,000 renovating each of them. So all we have to do is add the figures we used to illustrate the 15% tax credit to the ones we used to illustrate the 20% tax credit and we will have your total tax savings for the year. You save $17,000 for the 35-year-old project ($15,000 tax credit plus $2,000 on depreciation) and $21,-944 on the 40-year-old project ($20,000 tax credit plus $1,500 on depreciation). Between the two projects you save yourself $38,944. This is the actual amount that you chop off your final tax bill after taking all your other deductions.

Now you have a remaining tax bill of $25,000 for the year and $38,944 in tax credits to apply against that bill. Since you can't reduce your taxable income to less than zero, you actually have more tax shelter than you need, a lot more—$13,944 more than you need, to be exact. You don't want all that tax shelter to go to waste, but I've already said you can't reduce your taxable income to less than zero, so what do you do with it?

Fortunately, there is an easy answer. You can carry that loss back up to three years and get a refund on taxes that you have already paid, or you can carry it up to seven years into the future and not have to pay tax on your future earnings. There is no reason why it should go to waste. In fact, if you don't need that extra tax shelter at all, you can always sell it to those who do, but we'll get into that in a later section.

THE FIVE-YEAR DEPRECIATION SCHEDULE

Normally, real estate must either be depreciated using the straight-line method, which means that you depreciate the property by the same amount each year for the next 18 years, or the accelerated declining-balance method, which gives you increased benefits the first few years, but then penalizes you later, especially when you sell the property and have to deal with recapture. Some of the HUD-sponsored rehab programs give you another choice: Instead of taking a 15% or 20% tax credit the first year and then having to depreciate the property over the next 17 years using the straight-line method, you can depreciate the property in only five years instead. This cuts down your tax benefits the first year, but gives you increased benefits in the remaining four years.

For example, if we assume that your HUD-approved project is at least 40 years old and would qualify for the 20% rehabilitation tax credit, it would work out something like this: If you take the tax credit, your first year's tax saving will be $21,944. That is the positive side. The negative side is that the second year you get no tax credit. All you get is $3,888 worth of depreciation. Since you are in the 50% tax bracket, you would save $2,333.33 the second year and for each of the following 16 years, assuming that you hold the property until the depreciation runs out. If you take the five-year depreciation schedule instead, you would base the depreciation on a figure of $80,000 instead of $70,000, since you would not have to deduct half the $20,000 tax credit.

If you divide $80,000 by five years, you get $16,000. This is the amount of depreciation you get the first year and each of the four years after that. Since you are in the 50% tax bracket, you save $8,000 in taxes. This is a loss of $13,944 in tax savings the first year, but then, each of the next four years, you would get an extra $6,056 in tax savings over and above what you would have gotten if you had taken the 20% tax credit instead of the five-year depreciation schedule.

If you multiply $6,056 times four years, you get a total of $24,224. This is the total of the extra tax savings you would have over the four-year period. It more than offsets the $13,944 in extra tax benefits you lost the first year. Whether this means you are wiser to take the five-year depreciation schedule instead of the tax credit depends on your individual situation.

WHEN YOU NEED THE TAX SHELTER

You have to decide how badly you need the tax shelter the first year and balance that against the amount of tax shelter you feel you will need in following years, and your chances of getting it. If you expect to keep doing renovation projects on a regular basis, you are probably better off taking the tax credits.

Remember, if you don't need all that tax write-off yourself, you can always sell it to someone who does, and we are going to talk about how to go about it in a later chapter. On the other hand, if you don't expect to be doing renovation projects on a regular basis and you do expect to need tax shelter in subsequent years, maybe you would be better off taking the five-year depreciation schedule.

Remember too that our comparison test was based on the idea of a 20% tax credit, but if your project is less than 40 years old, you will only get a 15% tax credit. This alone could easily tip the scales in favor of the five-year depreciation schedule instead. The final thing you must remember is that only certain HUD-approved projects qualify for the special five-year depreciation schedule.

Any non-residential rehab project that is at least 30 years old can qualify for a rehabilitation tax credit. Therefore, you may not even have a choice. If the HUD quotas are all filled up in your area, you may not be able to use the special five-year depreciation schedule anyway. To fully avail yourself of any or all of these programs, you should check with HUD, the IRS, and your accountant or tax advisor to make sure you are getting the maximum benefits you are entitled to. But, for now, let's run through them once again quickly, and then go on to some new ways to make money.

KEY POINTS TO REMEMBER

1. The 15% Rehabilitation Tax Credit

To qualify for this program you must buy and renovate a non-residential property that is at least 30 years old, or a residential property specially designated and approved by HUD for low-income housing. The tax credit is for 15% of the renovation cost and does not include the cost of purchasing the property. One-half of the amount of the tax credit must then be deducted from the basis used for depreciating the property. Only straight-line 18-year depreciation may be used.

2. The 20% Rehabilitation Tax Credit

The rules are the same as they are for the 15% tax credit, except that the building must be at least 40 years old.

3. The Special Five-Year Depreciation Schedule

This option is available only with certain HUD projects for low-income renters. Instead of taking a rehabilitation tax credit, you can depreciate the property in only five years.

CHAPTER TWELVE

REHABILITATION LOANS and OTHER GOODIES

REHAB RICHES

In addition to the loan programs HUD and the FmHA offer to prospective homebuyers and investors, there are also programs specifically aimed at homeowners/homebuyers and investors who want to get into rehabilitating older, run down, but potentially salvageable properties. It is those programs that we are going to cover in this chapter. Some of these programs are strictly for homeowners/homebuyers, while others are open to investors, and nonprofit developers as well, so we are going to start with the homeowners and would-be homeowners programs and then go on from there to the investor-oriented programs.

REHABILITATION MORTGAGE INSURANCE
(REVISED SECTION 203(K) (FHA))

This program provides insurance for one- to four-unit properties. HUD insures loans to finance the rehabilitation of existing properties, to finance the rehabilitation and refinancing of existing properties, and to finance the purchase and rehabilitation of properties.

The maximum amount for these loans is the same as for standard FHA (Section 203(b)) homebuyers loans and anyone who is able to make the necessary cash investment and the mortgage payments is eligible. There are no restrictions on income or assets. The basic difference between this program and the standard HUD/FHA homebuyer and investor programs is that the properties are exempt from the normal requirement that they be up to HUD/FHA standards at the close of escrow. Normally, all necessary work must be completed and the property must be up to HUD/FHA standards before the loan will be funded. Since these standards are very strict, this eliminates many properties.

The Section 203(k) program allows these properties to be purchased "as is" and then brought up to HUD/FHA standards afterwards. The appraisal is based on the estimated value after the fix-up work has been completed and so the buyer gets one loan to cover the purchase and rehab work, with the specific requirement that the work be done according to HUD guidelines.

URBAN HOMESTEADING

This is a national program to revitalize declining neighborhoods and at the same time reduce the inventory of federally owned properties. The idea is to transfer these properties to qualified would-be homeowners who will live in them and rehabilitate them. The program cuts across departmental lines, and suitable properties owned by HUD, the Veterans Administration, and the Farmers Home Administration (Department of Agriculture) can be used in this program.

Properties are not transferred directly to would-be homeowners. Rather, they are transferred first to local governments that have set up homesteading programs approved by HUD. Each locality submits an application for participation in the program including designating certain neighborhoods as Urban Homesteading Neighborhoods. Funds set aside for this program reimburse the federal agencies involved for the value of the properties that they transfer to the local governments.

The local governments then screen applicants for participation in the program and pass these properties on to qualified applicants for a nominal fee. The "homesteaders" who receive these properties must agree to live in them as their principal place of residence for at least three years and they must bring the properties up to local code standards within 18 months. The homesteaders can either do the work themselves or have it done by a contractor, but they must allow inspections of the property and the work in progress while the process is under way. Once the property has been brought up to the standard of the local code and the homesteaders have occupied it for three years, they get fee simple title (free and clear) to the property and it is theirs. (For more details, see your local or state Housing Authority and ask about the existence of an urban homesteading program in your area and exact rules for applying.)

Home Improvement Loan Insurance (Title I)

HUD insures loans to help property-owners make major and minor improvements, repairs, and alterations of individual homes and non-residential properties (whether owned or leased). Loans on single-family houses can go up to $17,500 and run for up to 15 years and 32 days. Loans on apartment buildings can go as high as $8,750 a unit or $43,750 for the entire building but must be repaid in no longer than 15 years exactly.

Title I loans may also be used to finance new construction for agricultural or other non-residential use, so this is a pretty broad program. Loans of $2,500 are generally unsecured personal loans. In some cases, the borrower can do the whole thing by mail, without even appearing in person. It's a very simple process.

When the loans are over $2,500, they are usually secured by a lien against the property, a second or third mortgage. This means that the borrower must go through a more formal application process and get title insurance, etc. Lenders will generally be reluctant to make these loans if there is already more than one loan against the property, or if there is not sufficient equity. HUD insures these loans, but the borrower must apply through local commercial lenders (banks and savings and loan associations), so the lenders set the rules for qualifying borrowers, as long as they follow basic HUD guidelines and don't discriminate.

In the case of leased property, the borrower must satisfy the lender as to the security of the lease and the borrower's equity, if any (the difference between the cost of the lease payments and the current market-value rent). Normally, only tenants with long-term leases giving them effective control over the property (i.e., the right to sublet, renovate, etc.) would qualify.

Once a loan has been granted, the borrower is more or less on his own. Although the money is meant for the construction and renovation of his property, he generally won't be required to produce receipts from contractors or workmen for the exact amounts spent. He can't just pocket the money and do nothing to the property, however. That would be asking for trouble. But the work can often be done for less than the loan amount and then the borrower can pocket the difference as a tax-free reward.

FARMERS HOME ADMINISTRATION (FmHA) REHABILITATION LOANS

The Farmers Home Administration (FmHA) makes rehabilitation loans available to property-owners in country areas and in towns of less than 20,000 people. These loans are available for homeowners as well as investors. They are similar to the HUD/FHA 203(k) loans. The property is appraised on the basis of its value once it has been rehabilitated, as well as its present value, and buyers are given money to rehabilitate the property along with the purchase money loan.

The borrower must submit plans for approval before receiving the loan and the property must be rehabilitated according to FmHA guidelines. The property must blend in with the existing environment and every effort must be made to make the completed rehabilitation aesthetically pleasing and to preserve open space, rather than filling it in.

The purpose of these loans is to preserve and restore decaying housing in rural areas. Individual projects can be approved relatively easily, but with large-scale projects the investor/developer must demonstrate the effect on the community-at-large and show the need for rehabilitated housing. Due to the nature of rural communities, it may be more complicated there than it would be in an urban area. The input of the local community will be more direct and more important in the final approval process, since the impact on the community will be greater.

Flexible Subsidy

This HUD program provides funds to assist the owners of private but federally assisted multi-family housing projects. It is specifically designed to help restore or maintain the financial and physical soundness of the affected projects, improve their management, and maintain them as homes for low- and moderate-income people.

The program provides immediate cash to pay for deferred maintenance, replace anything that needs replacing, and to clear up replacement reserve and operating deficits. In order to qualify for funds initially as well as to keep receiving funds on an ongoing basis, the owner must prove that he can provide management satisfactory to HUD.

This program is open to anyone who owns a project with a mortgage insured or held by HUD and subsidized under Sections 236, 221(d)(3), the Below Market Interest Rate program, or the Rent Supplement program. Nonprofit projects developed by state agencies and receiving HUD assistance under one of the above subsidy programs are also eligible, even if the mortgage is not insured by HUD.

REHABILITATION LOANS

These loans are made by HUD to finance rehabilitation of single-family and multi-family residential, mixed use, and non-residential properties in federally aided Community Development Block Grant and Urban Homesteading areas.

The maximum loan amount is $27,000 per unit for residential properties and $100,000 for non-residential properties, but the actual amount of any given loan may be less, depending on certain factors to be determined by HUD at the time of application. These loans are for a maximum term of 20 years and the interest rate will be 3% to 9% for single-family loans, depending on family income, and 5% to 9% for multi-family projects of five or more units, based on the level of private dollars being leveraged; the money may be used for insulation and installation of weatherization items and features, as well as more traditional rehabilitation work.

To qualify for one of these loans, you must own property in one of the federally aided neighborhoods in your area. You can also qualify for one of these loans even if you only lease property in one of the affected areas, but your lease must run for at least the maximum term of the loan. Either way—owner or lessee—you must show the ability to repay the loan, but preference is given to low- and moderate-income applicants.

To find out which neighborhoods, if any, have been designated as Community Development Block Grant or Urban Homesteading areas in your city or town, contact your local HUD office or your local Community Development Agency.

WRAP-UP AND RECAP OF GOVERNMENT REHABILITATION LOAN PROGRAMS

Now that we have gone through all the loan programs designed just for rehabbing existing properties, let's run through them again quickly and see what options are available to a property owner who wants to get some government help to get his property back into good shape.

1) **Rehabilitation Mortgage Insurance (Revised Section 203(k))**

   Under this program homeowners can borrow money to fix up a property they already own and/or to refinance it. They can also use the money to buy and then rehab a property they do not already own. The maximum loan amounts are the same as for the FHA 203(b) standard homebuyers loan. Anyone who can qualify for the loan is eligible to apply.

2) **Urban Homestead Program**

   Actually, this one is not even a loan program. If you are a low- or moderate-income family and your local community is participating in the program, you can get a house for almost nothing. You have to be willing to live in it as your primary residence for at least three years and bring it up to local code within 18 months. If you do, then it's yours, free and clear.

3) **Home Improvement Loan Insurance (Title I)**

   You can borrow up to $2,500 unsecured with just a personal note under this program. You can also borrow up to $17,500 to do work on a single-family house and take up to 15 years and 32 days to pay it back (these loans would be secured by a second mortgage or trust deed against the property because they are for more than $2,500), or up to $8,750 a unit or $43,750 for a whole building and pay it back within 15 years (exactly) if you have multi-family units.

4) Farmers Home Administration (FmHA) Rehabilitation Loans

FmHA makes loans for rehabilitating single-family homes and multi-family projects in country areas and towns of less than 20,000 people.

5) Rehabilitation Loans (HUD)

These loans are specifically to aid property-owners in federally aided Community Development and Urban Homesteading areas. If you qualify you can get loans for as little as 3% interest if you own a single-family home, and 5% interest if you own a multi-family property. To find out if your property is in one of these areas, contact your local HUD office or Community Development Agency.

6) Flexible Subsidy (HUD)

This program is for property-owners who have a multi-family moderate- to low-income project that is in physically or financially bad shape. If you can prove to HUD that you are capable of providing satisfactory management and your mortgage is insured under Sections 236, 221(d)(3), Below Market Interest Rate, or the Rent Supplement program, then you may be able to get immediate cash to help get you back on your feet, and non-financial management assistance as well.

KEY POINTS TO REMEMBER

1. Each government agency (HUD, VA, and FmHA) has its own rules for rehab projects.
2. HUD-approved rehab projects can qualify for special tax credits.
3. HUD-approved rehab projects can qualify for special depreciation schedules.
4. Funds for purchase and rehab can be packaged together.

CHAPTER 13

BILLIONS OF DOLLARS ARE WAITING FOR YOU

OPPORTUNITIES FOR INVESTORS

The government's main purpose is to help homebuyers and renters, but there are plenty of programs for investors as well. We live under the free enterprise system and it has been proven, time and time again, that the private sector can do things better than the government can.

This is why the government has so many incentives for investors—to get them involved in the type of housing that the government wants. There are special interest rates and special tax breaks for getting involved in housing for the elderly, the handicapped, low-income people, etc.

In order to qualify for these special benefits, you have to contact your local Housing Authority or Department of Housing and Urban

Development office and find out what types of programs are being funded in your area. Starting below is a survey of the programs available, but remember, they may not all be available in your area at all times.

MULTI-FAMILY RENTAL HOUSING (SECTION 207)

This program provides HUD insurance for a variety of purposes connected with rental housing. Both public and private developers can apply for funds to build or rehab rental projects of at least five units. The idea is to provide moderately priced rental housing for families with or without children, so the tenants (or prospective tenants) must include couples as well as singles, and the rents must be reasonable enough to accommodate them without pricing them out of the market.

The project must also be in an area that has been approved by HUD for rental housing and the market conditions in the area must show there is a need for moderately priced rental housing for families. Investors, builders, developers, and anyone else who is interested can apply to their local HUD office for details and then go to a lender that is FHA-approved for a loan. The program is administered by the office of the Assistant Secretary for Housing, Federal Housing Commissioner, Department of Housing and Urban Development, Washington, D.C. 20410.

EXISTING MULTI-FAMILY RENTAL HOUSING (SECTION 223(F))

This program provides HUD insurance to purchase or refinance existing rental housing of five units or more. It is open to developers, builders, investors, and anyone else who can qualify for HUD financing. The project does not have to have been insured by HUD in the past, as long as it also meets HUD standards and is at least three years old. The units can be in need of moderate rehabilitation, but nothing major (we have a different one for that). This program is also administered by the office of the Assistant Secretary for Housing, Federal Housing Commissioner, Department of Housing and Urban Development in Washington, D.C. 20410.

MULTI-FAMILY RENTAL HOUSING FOR LOW- AND MODERATE-INCOME FAMILIES (SECTION 221(d)(3) AND (4))

This is the program for apartment projects that require major rehabilitation. HUD will provide insurance for the construction or substantial rehabilitation of units for low- and moderate-income families or for those who have been displaced by urban renewal. The financing can be used for either rental or cooperative housing and the projects can be either apartments or detached or semi-detached cottages and houses. There is no break on the interest rate. The loans are insured at the maximum interest rate for FHA loans, but there is a legal limit on the dollar amount per unit so the cost can be kept down.

If the units are occupied by eligible low-income families, the projects can qualify for Section 8 assistance. Actually, these are two separate but similar programs with slightly different rules. HUD can insure 100% of the total project cost for nonprofit and cooperative mortgagors under Section 221 (d) (3), while under Section 221 (d) (4), HUD can only insure mortgages for 90%. Section 221 (d) (4) also used to offer interest subsidies to bring the interest rate down as low as 3%, but those have been eliminated, along with rent supplements.

Mortgages insured under Section 221 (d) (3) are available to public agencies, nonprofit, limited-dividend, or cooperative organizations, and private builders or investors who sell their completed housing projects to such organizations. Loans insured under Section 221 (d) (4) are also available to all these groups as well as to profit-oriented sponsors who intend to hold on to the projects and run them themselves. There are no restrictions on the income level of the tenants or proposed tenants except in the case of those who are receiving subsidies.

MORTGAGE INSURANCE FOR HOUSING FOR THE ELDERLY (SECTION 231)

This program provides HUD insurance for rental housing for senior citizens and individuals who are handicapped. The funds can be used to build or rehabilitate multi-family projects with at least eight units. Any qualified person or group can get mortgage insurance under this program: investors, developers, builders, public agencies, and nonprofit organizations.

There is no restriction on who the tenants must be, as long as they are at least 62 years old or handicapped. Income, assets, etc., do not count in determining eligibility.

NURSING HOMES AND INTERMEDIATE CARE FACILITIES
(SECTION 232)

If you are an investor, builder, developer, or a representative of a non-profit corporation or association that is licensed or regulated by your state government and allowed to run a care facility or nursing home, you may qualify for one of these loans. You can get HUD insurance to build or renovate facilities to care for 20 or more patients requiring either skilled nursing care (and related medical services) or constant surveillance and care by trained but non-licensed personnel.

You may combine nursing home and intermediate care services in the same facility or you may have them in separate facilities. Major equipment needed to operate may be included in the mortgage, along with facilities for day care. All persons requiring skilled or intermediate care are eligible to live in these facilities with no restrictions.

RURAL RENTAL HOUSING

The Farmers Home Administration makes loans to provide rental housing in rural areas of 10,000 people. (Those living in areas of 10,000 to 20,000 people may be able to participate in the program as well and should check with their local FmHA office.) Loans are made for building or buying, or repairing apartment-style housing usually consisting of duplexes, triplexes, etc., as well as garden apartments and other multi-family projects. The housing must be modest in size and cost but adequate to meet the tenants' needs.

The loan money can also be used to buy and improve the land on which the rental housing will be located, to provide streets and water and waste disposal systems, to supply appropriate recreation and service facilities, and to install laundry facilities and equipment. Or you can use the money to landscape the property, including seeding lawns, planting trees and shrubs, or taking other measures to make the rental housing an attractive addition to the community. Is that broad enough for you?

About the only thing the loan money can't be used for, aside from fixing your Aunt Tillie's false teeth or buying your girlfriend a mink coat, is for any type of institutional housing. Aside from that, it's your money to spend.

WHO IS ELIGIBLE?

You should have the ability and experience to operate and manage a rental project successfully, but beyond that, just about anyone is eligible to apply for one of these loans: individuals, trusts, associations, partnerships, limited partnerships, nonprofit corporations and associations, as well as corporations organized for the purpose of earning a profit.

Borrowers must agree to provide rental housing for eligible low- and moderate-income families and they must show that they would be unable to finance the project with their own resources. With the exception of state and local public agencies, borrowers must prove that they are unable to obtain credit from other sources under terms and conditions that would permit them to rent to eligible low- and moderate-income families.

If the borrower is a profit or limited-profit organization, the assets of the individual members will be considered in determining whether other credit is available. These loans are to provide housing for rural residents, families with low- and moderate-incomes, and persons 62 and over.

The maximum income level for tenants will be established by FmHA. The maximum loan term is 50 years on projects designed for senior citizens and 40 years for all other projects. All applicants are required to provide operating capital equal to 2% of the cost of the project.

For nonprofit organizations and state or local agencies, the 2% operating capital may be included in the loan amount as part of the development cost. Loans to nonprofit organizations and state and local public agencies can be for 100% of the appraised value of the project or the actual development cost, whichever is less. Loans to all other applicants are for no more than 95% of the appraised value or the actual development cost, whichever is less.

Loans for the purchase of buildings one year old or less are limited to 80% of the appraised value. Before a loan can be approved, applicants must provide detailed plans, specifications, and cost estimates. They must provide complete architectural services, including inspections during construction. FmHA will review the plans and inspect construction as it progresses.

INTERIM CONSTRUCTION LOANS

Builders and developers who build their own projects may be permitted to earn the normal contractor's fee. How much this is will depend on the area and will be up to the county FmHA office to determine. All borrowers are encouraged to get interim construction loans from local

193

commercial lenders. In fact, borrowers have to show that no local construction loans are available through commercial lenders (banks, savings and loan institutions, and mortgage companies) before FmHA will make any construction loans. Borrowers have to wait until their loans close and authorization is given by FmHA before they start construction.

If they are using interim construction financing, they cannot start construction until the loan has been approved and the funds have been obligated. The local county supervisor of FmHA will provide information on how to complete and file applications. Applicants must furnish complete financial information, preliminary plans, specifications and cost estimates, a budget of anticipated income and expenses, and survey information supporting the idea that there is a need for housing in the area. You can get application forms and other sample FmHA forms for completing budgets and marketing surveys at your area or county FmHA office.

There are no fees for appraisals or for processing the loans, but you do have to pay for whatever legal work is involved to guarantee that you have a secure title to the property and any other incidental closing costs, such as escrow fees. These expenses can be included in the loan.

FmHA will hold a first mortgage (trust deed) against the property except if the borrower is a public or quasi-public organization which cannot give a real estate mortgage. In that case, FmHA will decide on alternative security for the loan.

The stated purpose of these loans is to help provide decent homes in a suitable living environment for low- and moderate-income rural families. Therefore, in some cases, there will be a limit on the maximum rent the tenants can be charged. This is to insure that qualified low- and moderate-income families are able to afford the rents. Applications should be submitted at the Farmers Home Administration office in the county where the project will be located, and you can get further details there.

TAX-EXEMPT DEVELOPMENT BONDS

This is the equivalent to the subsidized loan program for first-time homebuyers, except that it's aimed at commercial property instead. Local governments raise money by issuing low-interest, tax-exempt revenue bonds. They then loan this money out at low interest rates to people who want to start new businesses or revitalize existing ones, or for the purchase or leasing of real estate and its renovation for commercial use.

Local authorities have discretion in administering the money and there has been a lot of heat on this program too. Some legal but morally questionable businesses have gotten low-interest loans and this has caused opposition. (For example, in one well-publicized case, local officials approved money for a business dealing in pornographic books and video tapes.) But there is still money available in many areas and many legitimate investors and business people benefit from this program. Check with your local city or county government for details.

KEY POINTS TO REMEMBER

Once again, we have gone through a chapter full of varied and confusing loan programs, so, just to make sure I haven't lost any of you along the way, let's run through all the important details on each of them one more time.

1. FHA Investor Loans

Under this program, investors can borrow up to 85% of the maximum loan amount for an owner-occupant. The loans are for four units or less and they are fixed-rate loans usually with a maximum loan term of 30 years.

2. Housing in Declining Neighborhoods (Section 223(e))

This is the one to apply for if your property is in an area where you could not normally get HUD-insured financing. If this sounds like your area, this program could be your salvation. As long as HUD decides that your property is "an acceptable risk," they will relax the rules for their normal loan programs and you will get your loan.

3. Multi-Family Rental Housing

If you own or plan to buy a multi-family housing project in an area that HUD has approved for rental housing and that shows a need for rental housing for low- and moderate-income people, you can apply at a local HUD-approved lender for a HUD-insured loan. Check with your local HUD office to see if your property and your area qualify.

4. Manufactured (Mobile) Home Parks (Section 207)

If you own or plan to build a mobile-home park consisting of five or more spaces, in an area approved by HUD, where market conditions show a need for such housing, HUD wants to help you. They will insure your mortgage obtained through a private HUD-approved lender. You can borrow up to $9,000 for each individual mobile-home space within each park. In high-cost areas, this may be increased up to $15,750 per space. Check with your local HUD office to see if your property qualifies.

5. Existing Multi-Family Rental Housing (Section 223 (f))

If you want to buy or refinance an existing multi-family housing project of five units or more, you may be able to get an insured mortgage through HUD. The project must be at least three years old and not in need of any substantial rehabilitation. Apply at your local HUD office.

196

6. Multi-Family Rental Housing for Low- and Moderate-Income Families (Section 221(d)(3) and (4))

If you plan to build or substantially rehab a rental or co-op project, HUD will insure your loan under this program and you can even get up to a 90% loan. If the units are occupied by eligible low-income families, you can also get Section 8 assistance.

7. Lower-Income Rental Assistance (Section 8)

Under the Section 8 program you can fill up a building you already own (or single-family rental houses) with qualified low-income tenants and let HUD subsidize their rents and be responsible for any damage they might do to your property. Or you can buy a building to rehab (or rehab one you already own) and sign a 15-year lease with HUD or your local Housing Authority and get automatic rent increases each year and guaranteed rents even when you have a vacancy. And this is supposed to be a program to benefit tenants!

8. Mortgage Insurance for Housing the Elderly

If you want to build eight or more units for the elderly or handicapped or rehab eight or more units that you already own (to make them suitable for the elderly or handicapped), HUD will help out by offering mortgage insurance to make it easy for you to get a loan. Check with your local HUD office.

9. Nursing Home and Intermediate Care Facilities (Section 232)

If you are building or renovating a nursing home or intermediate care facility for 20 or more people, this HUD-insured loan program should make it easier for you to get financing. Check with your local HUD office or your lender.

197

CHAPTER FOURTEEN

THE 25% TAX CREDIT: MINING AMERICA'S RICH HERITAGE FOR FUN AND PROFIT

THE MOST PROFITABLE PROGRAM

This is the most profitable of all of the government's tax incentive programs for real estate. It is also the most complex and difficult to qualify for; that is why I decided it was necessary to devote a whole chapter to it. In fact, qualifying for the 25% Rehabilitation Tax Credit for Historically Certified Properties involves two distinct processes, so it almost deserves two chapters all to itself.

First, you must get the property approved for and added to the National Register of Historic Places. That is step one. If the property is not eligible for the National Register, there is no way you can qualify the project for the 25% Rehabilitation Tax Credit. You may as well give up and settle for the 15% or 20% tax credit instead. There is no point in even going on to step two.

If the property does qualify for the National Register, you must get your plans for the rehabbing and renovation approved by the Department of the Interior. This is step two. If the Department of the Interior turns down your plans, you have to redo them. They are in charge, and if you do not qualify, you will not be approved for the special 25% Rehabilitation Tax Credit for Historically Certified Properties.

HOW TO QUALIFY

Now that you know the basic rules of the game, let's get down to the serious business: What do you have to do to qualify? How do you get your property on the National Register, and then, how do you get your project approved? Fortunately, there are some relatively simple guidelines to follow.

First, to get your property on the National Register, you have to prove it is of historical significance. That's another one of those nice, vague, bureaucratic terms that don't tell you much. What is "historical significance"? It is different things to different people, so the rules start out by telling you what it isn't.

Historically significant properties are not the homes of historical figures. They are properties that are significant for themselves, not on account of their former occupants. They are not normally graveyards or religious sites, either. Or the gravesites of historical figures, properties owned by religious institutions or used for religious purposes, structures that have been moved from their original locations, reconstructed historic buildings, properties primarily commemorative in nature, or those which have achieved significance within the last 50 years. Prop-

199

erties such as these will qualify only if they are integral parts of certified historical districts or if they are exceptional for some other reason.

Establishing Historical Significance

What will qualify for the National Register of Historic Places are properties that are original examples of historically significant architectural designs on styles (e.g., Southern or New England Colonial, Southwestern Spanish style, New York Brownstone, etc.). Or properties that are associated with events that have made a significant contribution to the broad patterns of our history or are associated in some way with the lives of people significant in our past, or finally, properties that have given us, or are likely to give us, important information about our past history or prehistory.

For example, let's say you have a property that is not particularly noteworthy for its architectural style but was an important part of the economic or cultural history of the region, state, or local area. You could then apply for historical certification on that basis alone. Maybe it was a central marketplace that contributed significantly to the development of commerce, or the first county courthouse in the state, or the original home of the state's first governor, etc.

It does not even have to have occupied a famous or prominent place in history. For example, it might be the last livery stable to remain in business after the advent of the automobile or the last of the original one-room schoolhouses, or even a collection of old warehouses.

As long as you can show the historical significance and the need to preserve it as part of local, state or national history, you can apply to your local or state historical society for nomination to the National Register of Historic Places. If the state or local historical society agrees that your property has historical significance, they will nominate it for inclusion in the National Register and forward your application to the Department of the Interior.

DOES IT SERVE THE PUBLIC INTEREST?

The burden is on you every step of the way. You must show how and why the property in question meets the criteria of historical significance. Why is it special and why is it in need of special protection in order to preserve it?

How will the public interest be served by certifying the property as historically significant? As I said at the end of the last section, this program is not as easy as the others to qualify for, because no one is trying to make it easy for you.

In fact, you might ask yourself if it is even worth it to you to fool around with this program at all. You are saving only 5% of the cost of the rehabilitation work—over and above the 20% Rehabilitation Tax Credit you could have earned by renovating any non-residential building that was more than 40 years old—and in order to do it, you have to fill out all sorts of paperwork and put up with the whole bureaucratic process to a much greater degree.

WHY BOTHER WITH HISTORICALLY CERTIFIED PROPERTIES?

Is it worth it? That depends on your outlook and the size of your project. If it is a single-family house where you expect to spend $10,000 on renovations, the answer may very well be no. After all, you are only talking about a difference of $500 between a 20% tax credit and a 25% tax credit, anyway. It is really worth it to go through the whole process just to save $500 on your taxes? Not unless you are desperate.

But what if you could save $50,000? Or half a million? What if you are renovating a whole complex of buildings and plan to spend $100 million on renovation costs alone? Would it be worth it to fill out some forms and put up with some additional bureaucratic mumbo jumbo for $5,000,000 worth of tax credits?

You have to assess your own situation as well as the property and the area. Decide what your chances are to get the property historically certified and then balance the reward—an extra 5% tax credit—against the punishment of getting the property and your renovation plans approved by the Department of the Interior. Then decide for yourself if it is worth it to you.

HISTORIC CERTIFICATION CONSULTANTS

Some people who are planning large projects they need certified hire consultants just to help them fill out all the paperwork. This usually costs anywhere from $3,000 to $10,000 or more depending on the size of the project and the complexity of the application, but it can be well worth it.

If you don't fill in the application properly, it won't get approved, even if the property and plans would ordinarily qualify. You have to give the bureaucrats what they want, because they are the ones with the power to say yes or no. They make the guidelines and they enforce them. You can only take orders and learn how to play the game, if you want to save money on your taxes, because that is how it is done.

The old saying tells us that one picture is worth a thousand words, but when dealing with historical properties, you have to use pictures and words. In fact, you have to use words to create pictures.

Say It with Pictures

Instead of telling the examiners that your property has historical significance, you must tell them why it has historical significance, or better yet, show them with stories and pictures so that they can see it clearly for themselves and don't have to take your word for it. This way, you don't have to convince them. They convince themselves. This is what the consultants should be doing for you. They are usually ex-bureaucrats themselves or else people who know how to deal with the bureaucracy because it is their everyday job.

For you, it is only a once-in-a-while experience, so you are not likely to be as smooth or polished as they are in these matters. You don't want your application to be full of boring, irrelevant details that have nothing to do with the property's eligibility. Even bureaucrats have their limits, and boring irrelevant applications only make them hostile.

Details Count

On the other hand, you do want to include every detail that is relevant and possibly important. You want to make sure nothing is left out. The one thing you miss might be the one thing that prevents your getting approval, so you want to make sure that you get it all. But how do you know what to include and what to leave out? It takes experience and if you haven't got that and you can't afford to hire a consultant who does, you have to rely on common sense. Just picture them asking you a series of questions.

What questions are they likely to ask? What answers can you give to help establish the historical significance of the property? For example, put yourself in the position of one of the people reviewing the nomination forms and ask yourself which of the two following nomination forms you would be likely to look favorably upon and why. Keep in mind that "significance" is only one category of many to be filled out, but it is a very important category, probably the only truly important one in determining whether or not the nomination is approved.

NOMINATION FORM NUMBER ONE: THE WALLACE WINDBAG HOUSE, ANYTOWN, U.S.A.

The Wallace Windbag House is the house where I grew up and where I still live, so I am more than intimately acquainted with its historical significance. Not only was it built before World War II, but my parents were married there along with my aunts Lucille and Millie, and my Uncle Joe.

The house was built for my grandfather by some contractor whose name escapes me, but he was very old even then and I'm sure he had a lot to do with the town history and built lots of other houses besides my grandfather's place. It is three stories high, not even counting the attic, and was one of the first houses in the neighborhood to be fitted with a TV antenna on the roof. We watched the beginnings of "The Ed Sullivan Show" and "I Love Lucy"—the first episodes—right here in this living room when I was a child. Those were historic events and I will never forget them.

The house has been in the Windbag family through three wars (World War II, Korea, and Vietnam) and while, of course, none were fought in this country or had any direct bearing on local history, they were historical events that this house has witnessed.

As for local history, the Windbags are very prominent in local history for a variety of reasons. Just ask any Windbag and he will be glad to recite for you our accomplishments, achievements, awards, accolades, and attainments in and around Anytown and the fact that Old Grampa Wallace Windbag's house has always been the family seat.

During our time here, the years we have been living in this house, Anytown has grown from a small town of only 250,000 people to a thriving metropolis of at least 275,000 and it has gone through enormous change and historical development. Why, it's at least 15 years now since they widened the street we live on and made it two ways instead of one. You're part of history before you even know it.

NOMINATION FORM NUMBER TWO: THE RIVERFRONT WAREHOUSE DISTRICT, ANYTOWN, U.S.A.

The Warehouse District sprang up between 1830 and 1860 in the years just prior to the Civil War. Before that time, Anytown had been primarily a small town river port and secondary cattle market town. The main sources of income were cattle raising and trading, occasional small farming, and catering to the river boats that passed through on their way south. Saloons, gambling dens, and brothels were the town's primary establishments and it was known as a wide-open town.

The first known warehouses along the river front were put up by Henry Peterson, who went on to become the town's first real mayor and served in office until his death in 1863. He designed the buildings in the style now known as Anytown Late Pioneer, with low sweeping lines and large, latticed windows facing the river. This style was just coming into vogue about 1830–1835, and it dominated much of the commercial-industrial architectural planning in Anytown for at least the next 40 years, and might have gone on longer if it were not for the Civil War.

The buildings in question are all original examples of this historic style. They show clearly what commercial-industrial architecture was like in this important and formative period in Anytown's history.

The Warehouse District is also significant because of its role in Anytown's development. Prior to the 1830s the town was just a backwater river port. After 1830, the development of the warehouses allowed the town to mature into a regional market center. Produce and commodities from the surrounding area were brought to town, stored in the warehouse, and then moved downriver by boat. Likewise, merchandise brought in by boat was stored right there by the river until it could be sold or distributed inland. This greatly affected not only Anytown's status, but the status of the entire region as increased trade attracted new population and new industries.

Gradually, the whole region changed from ranching to farming and trading as its main sources of economic livelihood. The development of permanent storage facilities along the river front was absolutely essential to this change and helped Anytown to grow from a town of less than 5,000 people to a small city of over 50,000 in only 30 years.

The Warehouse District also played an important part in the Civil War, when the warehouses were used to store supplies essential to the war effort, particularly in the famous siege of Anytown in 1864; most historians agree that the supplies stored in the warehouse district were the only thing that enabled the local militia to hold out for as long as they did until reinforcements arrived.

The district continued to be an important factor in the economic life of the entire region until recent years when the combined rise of the container shipping revolution and the increasing use of truck, rail, and air transportation diminished its economic, but not its historical, significance. As a result, many of the finest old buildings are now starting to fall into a state of disrepair.

Those still in use are generally rented for industrial use or as permanent low-cost storage areas by local families and small businesses, which have neither the resources nor the serious inclination to maintain them properly without special incentives to do so.

Not a Chance

You don't have to be very experienced with this program to realize that the second application form has a much better chance of being accepted. The second application form pretty much says it all, while the first one says virtually nothing. If there is any real historical significance to the Wallace Windbag House, the applicant has done a fairly good job of keeping it a secret.

The application is filled with details, but most of them don't tell anyone anything important about the property. The main reason for the application seems to be that the applicant wants the tax credit, but unfortunately, that is not reason enough.

What of historical significance did old Wallace Windbag himself have? The grandson who now occupies the house tells us he was a prominent citizen but offers no proof. There is not one example of anything he did, not one story or one concrete accomplishment listed to back up this claim. If he was a prominent, historically significant person, then his heirs should not have any trouble documenting that fact with a list of his deeds and their historical importance.

As for the house itself, the application form clearly states that the historic events mentioned took place nowhere near the house and did not affect the house in any way, nor were they affected by it. The fact that the house was in existence while these historic events were taking place is not enough to give the house itself any historical significance, even if they had taken place in the immediate area instead of on the other side of the world.

WHY THIS COULD SUCCEED

The second application, on the other hand, clearly and concisely states exactly what the historical significance is, both for the Warehouse District itself and for the founder of the Warehouse District, Henry Peterson. This way, we get a clear picture of the architectural significance of the district as an example of a unique and historically important architectural style representative of a particular time period. This is argument number one in favor of its historic importance.

Next, we are shown the connection between the river front Warehouse District and the life of an important figure, the town's first real mayor, who served for over 30 years. The length of his term in office is as significant as the fact that he was the first mayor because it shows that his influence on the growth of the town was long-standing. This gives the Warehouse District added importance because of its role in the political as well as economic history of the town.

Then we are given a detailed account of the role the Warehouse District played in the economic and population growth of the town and surrounding area. Assuming the information stated in the nomination form is accurate and is based on facts, how could anyone doubt that the Warehouse District played an important historical role in the development of Anytown into an important regional population center?

Also, the application ties in the important event in the history of Anytown—the Civil War—and shows how the war did affect the Warehouse District and the Warehouse District did have an effect on and involvement in the war. This adds one more bit of evidence. If the property does not qualify on any other grounds, then it could be declared a Civil War monument. This alone should qualify it for inclusion in the National Register of Historic Places.

Finally, just to tie everything together neatly, the second application gives the reason why these historically significant properties need special protection: They have declined in value and are no longer being kept up and will not be kept up unless they are given special protection. This is important, because the program we are dealing with here is officially known as the Historic Preservation Ordinance.

REMEMBER THE PURPOSE

The purpose is not just to issue special Rehabilitation Tax Credits to worthy investors and property-owners, but to help preserve historically significant properties that would otherwise be in danger of deterioration or demolition. If you can show that the property in question is in need of special protection, the nomination examiners will take this into consideration.

Another thing that can also help your case immensely is reference to published sources. There is a special section on the nomination form for bibliographical information. If you can show published references to the building or district in question, in relation to historic events or persons, this will go a long way to help prove that the property is of historical importance.

But all of this, complex as it may seem, is only half the battle. Once you have the property added to the National Register of Historic Places, you still don't automatically get any tax credits. In order to do that, you still have to get your restoration plans approved and you must assure the Department of the Interior that you can accomplish all you intend to do without disturbing the architectural integrity of the property.

In one very real sense, you are over the largest hurdle by the time you get the property certified for inclusion in the National Register of Historic Places. But you still haven't qualified for the 25% tax credit. In fact, you have a long way to go, but at least from this point on, you control your own destiny.

What If You're Turned Down?

If your plans are turned down, you can always appeal. If that doesn't work, you can usually work out some sort of compromise. If that does not work, you can always give in and make your plans conform to what the Interior Department wants. You may not like the idea of doing this and it may even cost you some money to do it, but at least you know that, ultimately, your project will be approved if you are willing to compromise and alter your original plans.

If you lose out in the first stage of the process, however, you don't have that option. If your project is declared to be lacking in historical significance, you can appeal, but ultimately there is nothing you can do. There is no way you can modify the project to give it historical significance. It either has it or it doesn't.

Once it has been established that it does have historical significance, it is just a matter of proving to the Department of the Interior that your plans will help preserve that historical significance, rather than destroying or altering it in any way. How do you do this? With detailed plans accompanied by drawings and other documentation to show the present appearance and condition of the property, both interior and exterior.

Particularly relevant are any special features which might contribute to the architectural or historical significance of the property, since it is important to preserve these in their original condition. The only smart way to do this is to submit your plans for approval before you start the work. If you do the work first and then apply for certification, you are taking a very big chance that you will be turned down.

SUBMIT YOUR PLANS FIRST

If you submit your plans first, the Department of the Interior will work with you to help make those plans conform to their guidelines, making suggestions and changes as necessary. If you do the work first and then apply for approval, you are cutting yourself off from this input. By doing that, you are taking a risk. If you think you will have an easier time getting approval simply because the work is already done, forget it. The process simply doesn't work that way.

There are guidelines to follow and they don't call for being lenient to those who have already done the work. They must pass the same tests as those who apply beforehand. If they don't, they are turned down. It is as simple as that. What do the examiners look for? Evidence that you have a clear understanding of the architectural features, if any, that make the project historically significant and have a clear and workable plan for preserving those features as well as the overall architectural integrity of the project.

For example, they don't want you to take a building that is historically significant because of its particular architectural style and then modify that style in order to modernize the property. This is just what the Historic Preservation Ordinance is supposed to prevent. Even if the original style was rather plain and unattractive and your idea is to spruce it up and make it more ornate, add some charm and make it more attractive, you will be turned down.

The idea is not necessarily to improve these properties, but to preserve them and keep them in their historically accurate style as living reminders of our past history. You might even get turned down for painting the outside of a property that was originally unpainted brick. This happened to at least one unfortunate applicant. The rule is not to change anything that can be kept original.

STRUCTURAL CHANGES

You can, of course, make structural changes, particularly if they are necessary to preserve the building or buildings; no one is saying you have to follow original construction methods or use only original materials if modern methods or materials will work better. For example, you would not necessarily be expected to use lathe and plaster to repair interior walls. Sheetrock and wallboard are the commonly accepted substitutes for that outdated process and using them will make no difference to the historical integrity of the project.

Once they are covered over with plaster and paint, no one will know the difference anyway. It won't affect the appearance or style of the property. But if you were to take a property with the old-fashioned rounded ceilings and try to square them off, that would be a different story. Then you would be interfering with the basic stylistic integrity of the property; even if it would be easier and more efficient to do it that way, it would not be permitted. If the rounded ceilings were a feature peculiar to that particular property and not to any style or period, it might be another story, but the burden would be on you to show that this was the case and you were not in any way interfering with the historic character of the house.

This rule does not mean, however, that you cannot change the use or function of a historically certified property. As long as you preserve the architectural and historic character, you can do as you like with the function, even changing industrial or commercial property to residential use or vice versa.

It Must Produce Income

But remember: In order to qualify for the special Rehabilitation Tax Credit, the property must be used to produce income. You must rent it out. You cannot just use it as a residence. Within these guidelines, you actually have a lot of freedom to improvise.

For example, in Akron, Ohio, an old Quaker Oats plant has been turned into a Hilton Hotel and shopping complex, complete with luxury hotel suites in what used to be the grain silos and are now the hotel's twin towers. By preserving the rough quality of the original structures, not only were the developers able to meet the Department of the Interior's guidelines, they added to the charm of the finished project as well.

This project is not an exception. There are hundreds like it around the country—commercial buildings converted to apartments and condominiums, warehouses converted to fancy shops. In many cases, tenants will pay premium rents for these properties. Why? Because anyone can have their home or office in a modern building, but there is a certain mystique and charm about well-done historic restorations that newer buildings lack.

Therefore, the government is not the only one who will pay you to keep it original and you can probably make a lot of money even if you don't get the tax credit. But there is no reason why you shouldn't get it.

If you have come this far and gotten the building listed in the National Register of Historic Places, you are past the really hard part. The rest is relatively easy. Once again, you need to put in all the relevant details you can, just as you did with the application for the National Register of Historic Places. The more you tell them, the happier they will be and the better your chances of being approved.

First of all, they want to know the property address. If the property is in a National Historic District, put down the name of that district.

213

This can be found in the Federal Register at most public libraries if you do not know the area.

If your property is individually listed in the National Register of Historic Places, you can skip this whole section. But if your property is part of a Certified Historic District, but has not been individually certified as historically significant to the district, you must fill out the entire application. After you have stated the property address and the name of the historic district that it is part of, you must go on and describe the exterior of your property.

REMEMBER THE DETAILS

Be especially careful to list any distinctive architectural features, but also give the age of the property, the number of stories, type of construction (brick, wood frame, etc.), and any alterations previously made to the existing structure (with approximate dates), and list any distinctive interior features. When you have finished this, it is time for a statement on why the property is historically significant and why it is an important part of the historic district. After that, you must give your own name, address, and phone number, and sign and date Part One of the application.

To back up your application at this point, you must include photographs that show the condition of the property and the appearance before any rehabilitation work was done (assuming that you have been foolish enough to do the rehabilitation work beforehand). The photographs must be large enough to show architectural features clearly and be labeled with the property name and address and a brief description of what is being shown.

Finally, last but not least, you must include a map showing that the property is within the boundaries of the historic district. Then, it's on to Part Two, which everyone has to fill out whether their property is individually listed in the National Register of Historic Places or not.

Part Two of the application calls for the name and address of the property and the name of the Certified Historic District it is located in, if any. You must list the date of construction, if you know it, the approximate amount of existing floor space (in square feet), the type of construction, and the original use of the building.

You also have to provide information on the rehabilitation work you have already done, or hopefully, plan to do. They want to know the starting date of the project, the estimated completion date, the estimated cost of the rehabilitation work, and the proposed use for the building. You must also specify whether the project has already received any federal assistance, and if so, what the source was. You must indicate whether or not the architectural plans and specifications are available for review and give the architect's or developer's name and address, if applicable.

But we're not through yet. You also have to describe the rehabilitation work, including site work, alterations to the exterior and interior of the building, and any new construction. You want to take particular care to describe the effects of rehabilitation work on specific architectural features that may contribute to the property's historical significance. For any features like this which your project may have, you must describe the condition of the feature in the following terms:

1. good (needs minor repair)
2. fair (needs major repair)
3. poor (repair may not be feasible)
4. unrestorable (deteriorated beyond repair)
5. unknown (include photographs or sketches that show the feature described)

Explain It

Explain the nature and purpose of the work you intend to do on that feature and describe the effect on existing features (visual, structural, etc.); include drawings or sketches that show the rehab work and its effect on existing structures. You also have to provide photographs to show the existing condition of the property prior to rehabilitation and indicate where the work will be done. You also have to back up the photographs with sketches of planned alterations or new construction. The sketches must be detailed enough to show the work accurately and should include floor plans and sections and elevations when appropriate.

After that, it is just a matter of signing and dating your application and stating that you believe it meets the Interior Secretary's "Standards for Rehabilitation," and then it's all over but the waiting. And then you can learn to sell those tax benefits for cash, in the next chapter.

KEY POINTS TO REMEMBER

1. Certified historical renovations earn a tax credit equal to 25% of the rehabilitation work.
2. The property itself must be certified eligible for inclusion in the National Register of Historic Places.
3. The renovation must be approved and certified by the Department of the Interior.

4. The historical character of the property must be preserved.

5. If a property is in the National Register of Historic Places or in a Certified Historic District, there may be restrictions on what the owner can do to the property.

6. You cannot use accelerated depreciation if you take the tax credit for renovating a historically certified property. You must use straight-line depreciation.

7. The property may be residential or commercial, but it must be used as income property and not as a personal residence in order to qualify for the rehabilitation tax credit.

CHAPTER FIFTEEN

SHARING THE WEALTH: LIMITED PARTNERSHIPS, UNLIMITED OPPORTUNITY

PART OF THE PROFIT IS BETTER THAN NONE

What do you do when you find a great deal but you can't get the money to put it together? You find a partner or partners who can. Government-assisted programs are especially amenable to this approach for a couple of reasons. Learning to form and use partnerships can help you get the most from these programs and put even more money in your pocket than if you work alone.

First, partners can be extremely useful when dealing with government programs because a lot of money is often involved in buying and rehabbing the properties involved, particularly when you get into some of the larger projects, and the government can be awfully slow about coming up with the money when it is supposed to.

Therefore, it can really help if the entire financial burden is not on your shoulders alone. The other reason partnerships work so well with government loan programs is that there are often extra tax benefits to share. This means you can give the partners these tax benefits and keep more of the profit for yourself. You can even increase your own net profit just by selling some of the tax benefits for cash that you can put in your pocket. You can also use your partners' assets and financial statements to help you qualify for federally insured loans.

Remember, these are not poverty programs we are talking about. You must qualify for them by showing income and credit statements, etc. If you can't do this on your own, it will be nice to have partners who can. How do you find these partners and set up your partnerships? The same way that you would do it if you were seeking conventional or owner-assisted financing.

SPREAD THE WORD

Talk to your friends, relatives, and neighbors. Talk to people where you work or go to school. Join investment groups and let people know that you know where to find good deals and how to put them together. Once you convince people that you are reliable, trustworthy, and can make money for them, you will have no trouble attracting investors, and once you know you have investors and their money behind you, it should increase your confidence in dealing with sellers, lenders, and bureaucrats.

Simple Partnerships

You can form simple partnerships to start, where you take in one or more partners and then split the costs and the profits. The property can be bought and held in both your names or one of you can take title while the other one remains a silent partner. This is the easiest and simplest way to form a partnership, but it has its drawbacks. What if something goes wrong? You and your partner(s) will be personally liable. You can be held responsible for all debts that the partnership incurs. You will be personally liable for any money owed to contractors or subcontractors, lawyers, consultants, lenders, etc. Anyone who has anything to do with the property can come after you, including your partner(s).

Limited Partnerships

These are the main reasons for forming limited partnerships. They take the worry out of being close. Or at least some of it, anyway. If you are the general partner, it won't offer you much protection. You can still be sued if something goes wrong. But what it will do is protect your limited partners from bearing the burdens of your mistakes. They cannot be sued if anything goes wrong. All they can lose is the amount of money they put into the project. This is why it's called a limited partnership: because it limits the liability of the limited partners. It also limits their involvement in the project.

Limited partners are, by definition, silent partners. The general partner makes all the decisions and bears all the responsibility. He oversees the project, fills out all the necessary applications, and deals with anyone who has to be dealt with, from bureaucrats to contractors to subcontractors and inspectors. It is really his project. The limited partners just put up the money and take a limited risk.

This makes it a very attractive investment for some types of people. Doctors, lawyers and other high-powered, high-paid business and professional people don't necessarily have the time to invest for themselves. They are too wrapped up in their main business or profession and are making too much money at it to worry about anything else. But, at the same time, they all, especially shrewd business people, want their money to work for them.

A limited partnership is a perfect solution for a person with money to invest but no time. He doesn't have to get personally involved and he can't lose any more money than he puts up, so he can't get too badly burned. He doesn't have to worry about jeopardizing his other assets and investments if anything goes wrong.

TAX BENEFITS ATTRACT INVESTORS

When you throw in the tax benefits of investing in real estate, it is easy to see why real estate limited partnerships and syndications are one of the most popular and fastest growing investments around. Where else can the average small- to medium-size investor get all the benefits with so little liability? And remember, with many of these government programs, you are able to offer better than normal tax benefits, so you should be able to draw even more investors.

When you get 35 or more investors involved in one project, you have a syndication and you must be licensed by the Securities and Exchange Commission as a securities dealer. Different states have different rules on which projects have to be registered with state authorities and which requirements have to be met, so check your local laws. Limited partnerships also offer other advantages to you as the general partner, besides helping you to raise cash.

As the person who puts the whole project together, you would normally get a share of any eventual profits, even though you would not necessarily be required to put up the same amount of cash as each of the limited partners. In fact, you might not have to put up any cash at all.

For example, let's say you get nine people together, plus yourself, and you form a limited partnership. You are the general partner and the others are just limited partners. You will find the property, put the deal together, and arrange for the financing. They will each put up their credit rating and financial statement and $10,000 in cash. You will all share equally in the profits from any projects the limited partnership takes on. Everyone, including you, will get 10% of the profits, after the limited partners have each gotten back their original $10,000 investment.

How You Will Benefit

Your contribution will be your talent and your time. If you do your job well, you will make money for everyone, including yourself. For example, you take the $90,000 your limited partners put up and you buy a piece of property, rehabilitate it under one of the government programs, and then hold it for five years.

During that five-year period, you are giving the limited partners most of the tax benefits, both the normal ones and the special ones. Then, at the end of the five years, you sell the property and the original $90,000 has grown to $450,000. That is what is left over after all the expenses have been paid off, all the loans, all the commissions and sales expenses. You take $90,000 off the top and give that to the limited partners. That is their original investment. You are now left with $360,000. You divide it ten ways and you each get $36,000 as your cut of the profits.

This may not seem like much money for five years of work; after all, you had to put the whole project together, find the investors, deal with the seller, the lender, the government bureaucrats and the tenants, and then you have to wait five years for your money. But it's only your share of the profit you have to wait for. No one says you can't collect a monthly management fee in the meantime—putting together the project is one thing, but managing the project is an entirely different responsibility.

If you are going to do both, you deserve to be paid for doing both. There is no reason to do it otherwise. I am not in favor of gouging investors. That is not going to get you anywhere in the long run. But there is no point in undervaluing your own labor, either. If you can really put together profitable deals, you have a valuable skill and you deserve to be well paid for it.

Multiple Fees

Some people even use a series of interlocking companies to charge multiple fees, which are all deducted before the limited partners get their original investment back. For example, they will charge one fee as the general partner, their management company will charge a fee for managing the project, and their consulting company will charge a consultant's fee for advice on putting the deal together and selling it for a profit.

When the time comes to split that profit with the investors, there is nothing left, because the general partner's fees have eaten up all the profit. Personally, I do not approve of that idea, even though the limited partners frequently will not object too strongly as long as they are getting the majority of the tax write-offs. This is the main reason why many investors go into limited partnerships anyway. Profits are a secondary motivation.

As far as I am concerned, this is all the more reason to be totally honest with your investors. Let them know clearly and without any misunderstandings exactly what fees are involved and which ones go to you. If you have a good, strong presentation and, especially, if you have any sort of track record to show what you can do, you won't scare off any of the really serious investors this way. The majority of them will appreciate your honesty and professionalism and they will like the idea of knowing just what they are getting into.

FLAT FEE OR PERCENTAGE?

One extremely successful young friend of mine specializes in historic renovations. She has developed a good reputation in her field, and now charges a flat fee of $100,000 in advance, plus a percentage of the profits, for any project in which she acts as the general partner. This is in addition to management and contracting fees and any brokerage commission involved, yet she has a waiting list for clients. Her fee is a flat $100,000 for a project, no matter how many investors are involved, or how few. The more investors, the less each one has to contribute. If there are ten investors involved in a project, they would each put up $10,000, plus their share of any other expenses. If there is only one investor, he would pay $100,000.

Other people charge each individual investor a fee to participate in their projects, so the more investors they attract, the more money they get as an up-front fee. Sometimes this per-investor fee is arbitrarily set according to whatever the general partner thinks the traffic will bear, while at other times it is tied to the amount of tax write-offs the limited partners will get. For instance, the limited partners might agree to pay the general partner one dollar for every two dollars in tax write-offs they get from the project. This way, everyone comes out ahead except the IRS.

Or it might be worked out where the limited partners have a choice, depending on how much cash they have and how much tax write-off they need. For example, they might put up $10,000 each in exchange for 50% of the tax write-offs and $20,000 each for 95% of the tax benefits. There are many different ways in which it can be done.

INCORPORATING TO CUT LIABILITY

Getting a fee for being the general partner does not change the fact that a lot of liability and responsibility is on your shoulders, however. If anything goes wrong, the general partner takes the heat. This is where the idea of incorporation comes in.

If you as an individual are listed as the general partner, you as an individual are responsible for that project and you are responsible to your investors and limited partners. If there is a lawsuit, they come after you, and that includes all your personal and business assets that are unrelated to the project at hand. You can lose everything you already have if one deal goes bad. If a corporation is listed as the general partner, the corporation is the only responsible party if something goes wrong.

You, as an individual, are in the clear. If there is a lawsuit of any type, the only thing anyone can get is the assets of the corporation. Your assets remain safe and untouchable. You may be a stockholder of the corporation. In fact, you may be the only stockholder, but you are still not responsible for the corporation's debts or liabilities.

Legally, you and the corporation are two separate entities. Normally, the limited partnership will also be a corporation, but that will not protect you from liability as the general partner. You must protect yourself by forming your own corporation to act as the general partner. For example, you might form a corporation and call it Cash Poor Investments, Inc. This corporation would then act as general partner in any limited partnerships you form. Once you have Cash Poor Investments, Inc., set up, you go out looking for investors and suitable properties.

BLIND POOL PARTNERSHIPS

There are two ways to do this: Some general partners seek the investors first, getting them to commit their money on faith, before any specific properties have been chosen. This is known as a "blind pool" partnership or syndication, because the limited partners throw their money into a blind pool and trust you to find suitable properties.

It is hard to get people to do this unless you have already completed one or more successful projects that have made money. Without that, most investors will be reluctant to put up their money until they know something about the property you intend to buy and what you intend to do with it. This brings us to the other obvious alternative: finding the property first and then getting your investors together.

SPECIFIC PROPERTY POOLS

When you are just getting started, you will probably find it a lot easier to get people to invest with you when they know specifically what they will be investing in. Once you have a definite property lined up, not only can you show the investors plans and pictures and sketches, you can also show them profit and tax-savings projections as well as give them a clear idea of exactly what expenses are involved.

All in all, this makes a much neater, more impressive package than some vague figures on the type of property you hope to get, the profits and tax breaks you hope to get, etc. Put yourself in the investors' shoes and ask yourself which would be most likely to appeal to you. If you have a clear plan for attracting investors, this should include at least a sketchy profile of who your average investor is likely to be, what will attract him, and what will turn him off. Once you have this, it shouldn't be too hard to decide whether you are better off seeking the investors first, or first lining up the deal.

INVESTOR ATTITUDES

Of course, another factor may be the state of the market in your area. What sort of properties are available and how much competition is there? Are sellers likely to accept contingent offers and wait for you to line up investors? Or will they just sell their properties to other people who are prepared to move a bit more quickly than you are? This can be important to your decision, just as important as the attitude of the investors.

If you can't get the deals, you will never get the investors, because you will have nothing to offer them. Decisions, decisions . . . and one more decision to be made with a limited partnership is how to pay off the investors. Do you want to give them a cut of the profits or just guarantee them a flat rate of return, either in a definite dollar amount or in a definite rate of interest, no matter how much or how little money the project makes? You can make a lot more money by paying your investors a flat rate, but you can also lose a lot.

It all comes down to how much faith you have in yourself and how much money you expect to make on any given project. Of course, you also have to consider the attitudes of the investors: How are they going to like the idea of a flat rate? Will that make it easier or harder to raise money? You also have to think about what will happen if something goes wrong. What if the project is ultimately successful but it takes longer to get off the ground than you expected? What if you cannot pay the limited partners their dividends or interest payments on time? What do you do then?

"Well," you say, "it doesn't matter anyway, because the general partner who promised to make those payments wasn't me, it was the Cash Poor Investments Corporation. The corporation is liable for that money. I'm not responsible for it." Legally, this may be true, but what about morally?

And what about your reputation? Don't you think the investors will talk to other people and tell them who was behind the corporation that lost them money? Is that going to help your track record? Not very likely. And as the person behind the Cash Poor Investments Corporation, you could be personally, or even criminally, liable if you made any false statements to the investors (e.g., promising payments you should have known were not realistic). Therefore, you want to be very careful before guaranteeing any investor anything except an honest deal, especially when you are dealing with government programs.

Strategies for Using Partnerships and Corporations

So, now you should have a good idea of how partnerships and corporations can be used, together with government programs, to create wealth. Let's go back to our friends Bob and Betty Bluecollar again and see how they can use some of these ideas to their advantage.

First, they could use a simple partnership to help them buy their home. They could get an investor to put up all or part of the down payment money and maybe even part of the monthly expenses, in exchange for a share in the ownership and the tax benefits. This is not legal if they do it at the time they buy the house, but there is nothing preventing them from adding their partner's name to the title, or even transferring the entire title to the parner's name, once the escrow is closed. We will get into this subject in a later section.

Since government-sponsored loans are assumable, all kinds of nice things can be done with them. As long as you wait a decent interval after the close of escrow before you transfer title, and if you don't do it too often, most likely you will not have any trouble. Once the partner is on title, he can claim depreciation on his share of the property, since he doesn't live there. Bob and Betty cannot claim depreciation on their share of the house. Since it is their residence, they can take a deduction only for the amount of the interest they pay. But their partner can claim his share of the property as a rental, if the transaction is set up properly.

If Bob and Betty decide to move up and get into two to four units, they could have up to three partners who would live in the property with them. Or they could have investor partners on the same basis as they could with a single-family house (i.e., added to the title after the close of escrow). If they decide to move into investing in real estate, they might stay with simple partnerships or get into limited partnerships.

CHOOSING LIMITED PARTNERSHIPS

Let's assume they do get into limited partnerships and see what happens, how they would go about protecting themselves. Let's say they have gone through all the available government programs for their area and have decided to concentrate on one of two projects. One is a historic renovation that will give them a 25% tax credit to share with their investor partners. The other is an apartment complex that they intend to turn into housing for the elderly and handicapped. It will give them a choice between a 20% tax credit the first year, or a five-year depreciation schedule. Plus, they will get a HUD or Housing Authority contract guaranteeing the rents for 15 years, even when the apartments are vacant, with automatic 7% rent increases every year.

Most likely, the Housing Authority or HUD will also be able to help them get low-cost funds to rehabilitate the property and, in some cases, to purchase it as well. Therefore, they prefer the elderly/handicapped project, but they will take whichever project comes through first.

Let's say it turns out to be the elderly/handicapped project. Bob and Betty don't want to buy the property in their own name. They buy the property in the name of the Elderly and Handicapped Housing Development Corporation, a limited partnership. The general partner for the limited partnership is Cash Poor Investments, Inc., another corporation that Bob and Betty have set up. This way, when they sign anything, they sign only as officers and authorized representatives of Cash Poor Investments, Inc., general partner for the limited partnership known as the Elderly and Handicapped Housing Development Corporation.

Cash Poor Investments charges the limited partners a flat fee for participating in the project, plus a percentage of any profits when the property is eventually sold or refinanced—after the limited partners have all recovered their original investment. Cash Poor Investments may also charge the limited partnership itself a management fee. Or Bob and Betty may decide to set up a separate management company, at least on paper, or hire an actual outside management company, since they don't have much experience.

LIMITED LIABILITY

The limited partners will receive no guarantees. They will get their investment back before Cash Poor Investments gets anything more than the initial fee or the management fee, but they will not necessarily make a profit. In fact, they could lose money, but not more than they put up.

Their liability is limited to the amount they have invested. They would also be silent partners with no responsibility and no say in the way Cash Poor Investments runs things, unless they can prove clear incompetence or fraud. As employees of Cash Poor Investments, Inc., Bob and Betty could draw salaries. As stockholders, they could draw dividends. They would have to talk to their tax advisor to see what would work out best for them. Each case is different.

This whole scenario would be virtually the same if they had done the historical renovation project, except that the name of the general partner would be different—probably something like Historical Restoration and Development Corporation, a limited partnership. Aside from that, the procedure would be almost identical, but the tax benefits would be less. In spite of that, there is still plenty there for everyone, no matter what approach they choose to take. In the end, it is up to you. To find out what to do about it, go on to the next chapter.

KEY POINTS TO REMEMBER

1. With simple partnerships, all partners are equally responsible for the partnership's debts and liabilities.

2. With limited partnerships, the limited partners are only liable for the amount they invested.

3. With limited partnerships, the general partner can be held accountable for the partnership's liabilities and debts.

4. General partners can charge cash fees in addition to sharing in any profits.

5. General partners can also charge management fees.

6. A corporation is a separate legal entity from the stockholders.

7. A "blind pool" is when investors put up their money blindly, on faith, before the general partner has any property picked out to buy.

CHAPTER SIXTEEN

GO FOR THE GOLD

I'm proud of the fact that I've probably helped to create more million-aires than anyone else in the country. Go to any state and to most major cities and you'll find Lowry alumni groups, with self-made mil-lionaires among the members and more on their way.

But what happens to all the rest? What about all the people who have taken my seminar and then disappeared, never to be heard from again, or the others, who attend alumni group meetings for a few months or a year and then drop out? What happened to them?

They received the same instruction as those who went on to become wealthy and they paid the same fee to get it, so why don't they follow up on what they have learned? I have done surveys and studies to try to find out and it always comes down to the same thing: their motivation ran out and they lost interest. So then I started searching for a way to combat this problem.

Making money has never been my primary goal in offering my seminars to the public. Certainly, I make money from them, but I make my real money the same way I have for the past 20 years, by investing in real estate. The main purpose of the seminars is to share what I have learned with others and help them to prosper as I have done. I came here as an immigrant and this country has been good to me. This is my way to give something back.

Therefore, I am always searching for ways to improve the seminar and help the attendees increase their rate of success. I don't want people to take my seminars and then never use the information. I want them to succeed and that means having the necessary tools to insure their success and then putting those tools to use. This is why I got excited when I ran into one of my former seminar graduates and she told me about a radical new approach to learning and motivation.

In addition to being a successful real estate investor, Danielle Durant is a certified hypnotherapist on the staff of the Hypnosis Motivation Institute. I spoke to her about my seminars and the problem of those students who never put their knowledge to use. She responded by telling me about the role of the subconscious mind in programming people for success or failure. She said that this was the reason why most motivational programs had only a temporary rather than a lasting effect, since they dealt only with the conscious mind.

Unfortunately, she explained, there is a force in the human mind so powerful that it defies our desires and sabotages our will power. The subconscious holds absolute control over much of our lives—our actions, habits, likes, dislikes, abilities, health, success and failure.

It is almost impossible to reach the subconscious by using will power, reason, or positive thinking. It resists any direct efforts on the part of the conscious mind to control it or alter its limits. I told her that while I personally believed in the beneficial effects of hypnosis as a motivational tool and a vehicle for helping people to improve their lives on a one-to-one basis, I just didn't see how I could use it to help my students on their road to success and financial independence.

I didn't see how this could help motivate a room full of future investors. I had to find some other way to break down the motivational barriers and get people to take charge of their own lives. Otherwise, they would never get the full benefit of what they learned.

This is when she told me about Dr. John Kappas, the founder and director of the Hypnosis Motivation Institute. Ms. Durant explained that Dr. Kappas was a psychotherapist and hypnotherapist, as well as a self-made millionaire. She said that after more than 30 years of research into the problem of how to reprogram the subconscious mind for success, prosperity, and happiness, Dr. Kappas had come up with an amazing new program, called the Mental Bank Concept. His goal was to discover the common denominators that enabled certain individuals to consistently achieve high levels of excellence in all areas of their lives. He had written a book called *Success Is Not an Accident* and had created a Mental Bank seminar, which he had personally trained Ms. Durant to teach.

"But isn't this just another positive thinking seminar?" I asked.

"No, it is not!" she answered firmly. "Most motivational programs such as positive thinking (wishful thinking) rely on the conscious mind, only 12% of your total mind power.

"The Mental Bank Concept is the only program that teaches you to utilize and reprogram the other 88%, the powerful subconscious mind. The Mental Bank Concept takes over where positive thinking leaves off. With this revolutionary self-help concept, you can tap into the power of your subconscious mind and let it work for you. Success can become automatic—a foregone conclusion—no longer simply beyond your reach."

She sounded so excited and so totally committed and convinced of what she was saying that I decided I had to find out more about the program. She offered to introduce me to Dr. Kappas himself; I now consider that to be one of the most important meetings I have ever had in my life. Dr. Kappas turned out to be a truly remarkable man and he has had a profound influence on me and, through Danielle Durant and the Mental Bank Concept seminars, on thousands of my graduates.

I began by explaining to Dr. Kappas that my seminars and books provided my students with the tools, techniques, and knowledge, in other words, the vehicle for financial security and wealth. My concern was for those who did not take advantage of what they had learned.

"Behavior experts say," Dr. Kappas explained, "that only 5% of those over 30 years of age will ever better their current lifestyle before they die without changing their subconscious life script."

I asked him what he meant by a "life script." He replied:

> From day one of our lives our minds are being subconsciously programmed and conditioned. We consistently identify and study parents, siblings, friends, teachers, and we let their value systems, goals, limitations, and lifestyles serve as role models. In our formative years, ideas, words, and directions enter our subconscious without question. It's as if our minds are like sponges, soaking up impressions without the benefit of mature logic and reason. We call this "life scripting." Many people form limited life scripts that hold them back from the success they consciously desire.
>
> Most positive thinking and motivational programs are on the right track, but they don't go far enough. We've discovered that there are five major steps to reprogramming your life script, but none of the existing motivational seminars or books covers more than two of them. We found this out by studying all the motivational and positive thinking programs to see where they went wrong, why they weren't more effective. We learned from their mistakes and this is why the Mental Bank Concept is the only one to take you through all five steps.
>
> There is virtually no limit to what the mind can conceive, and what the mind conceives, it will achieve, but positive thinking isn't going to change your life. It will make you feel good, but that only affects your conscious mind, not your subconscious and so it has no lasting effect. We all know people with negative attitudes who are successful in spite of their outlook, and positive thinking people who never seem to get ahead. Wanting to change your life isn't enough, because desire is conscious, but motivation is subconscious. This is the power of the Mental Bank Concept. It works where other motivational and success programs have failed, because it works with the subconscious rather than against it.

We talked for a long time and the more Dr. Kappas spoke, the more sense it made. The next time Ms. Durant taught the seminar, I sat in and found out it was everything she and Dr. Kappas had said it was—and more. In fact, the Mental Bank Concept is unlike any program I had ever encountered before. It allows people to make permanent changes in behavior, not just cosmetic changes or quick bursts of motivational enthusiasm that wear off after a few weeks or months. Most important, it is the only program that I know of that focuses on all three areas where most people would like to see an improvement in their lives: success, prosperity, and happiness. Some people are successful in their career or business, but it doesn't necessarily mean that they have achieved either prosperity or happiness in their personal lives and their relationships with other people. They may be highly respected, without being highly paid. Or they may be highly paid, but still feel as though they are not truly successful or happy.

Most seminars try to attack only one, for at most, two of these problems. The Mental Bank concept is the only success and motivational program I have ever heard of that can show you how to achieve all three: success, prosperity, and happiness. It can literally transform your entire life.

I knew immediately that this was what I had been looking for to help motivate my students. I made arrangements with Dr. Kappas and Danielle Durant to have Ms. Durant offer Mental Bank Concept seminars to the Lowry alumni groups, for graduates of my seminars. The results have been nothing short of astounding. She has taught the seminar to thousands of Lowry graduates all across the United States and the testimonial letters are very gratifying. People write to thank us and tell us how the Mental Bank Concept has changed their lives beyond their wildest dreams.

(For further information on the Mental Bank Concept, write to: Mental Bank, P.O. Box 6848 Westlake Village, California 91362 and start reprogramming your life script for success.)

READY, SET, GO. This book has now given you the inside track on how to make money in real estate with the government's help. You should be ready to grab the gold ring. That's an exciting thought, isn't it? There is nothing stopping you at this point, except yourself. Nothing at all.

SUCCESS STORIES always make me feel good, and each year I hear hundreds of them. Over the past 15 years, I have helped thousands of people to achieve financial independence. I have shown them how to solve their financial problems and make their dreams come true. I have received countless letters from grateful graduates of my seminars. They write to thank me and to give me the details of their successes. This is how I know that almost anyone can do it and that my own success is not unique.

Over the years, students have come to my seminars from a variety of backgrounds. We have had everyone from successful entrepreneurs and business executives to the hard-core unemployed. Old people, young people, rich and poor. They come to find out if the Lowry method really works, to see if investing in real estate can do for them what it has done for me, and they find that, yes, the Lowry method works, but only if they are willing to work.

SUCCESS IS NOT A MATTER OF LUCK. Mine wasn't. I worked and planned for it. I didn't just sit around hoping things would get better for myself and my family. If I had done that, I would probably still be cutting up pork chops for $5 an hour—when I could find work.

YOU DESERVE MORE OUT OF LIFE and I decided I did too. I felt I deserved more and I was determined to get it. I knew that other people were getting it. I could see them driving fancy cars, wearing fine clothes, going home to nice big houses, while I rode the bus back to my dinky one-bedroom apartment.

I decided I was meant to live the way the rich people were living and that was my first step toward success. You were meant to live like a rich person too. Why not? Aren't you as good as they are? So why shouldn't you get to live the way they do? You should. Now the only question is, What are you going to do about it?

The fact that you read this book in the first place shows that you want something more, but are you really willing to work for it?

Yes, There is Some Work Involved. That's right, work. This is not some flim-flam, get-rich-quick scheme we're talking about. It's a serious, down-to-earth business. It requires some effort on your part, effort and commitment.

It's not something you can fool around with for the next six months or so, before drifting on to something else. You have to be prepared to stick around for the long haul.

It's Called Get Rich Quick S-L-O-W-L-Y. Using the information in this book, it may take you up to three years or more to achieve financial independence—if you work at it conscientiously. That is exciting. Three years to financial independence, instead of 40 or 50 years of just working for a living.

Winner Or Loser, the choice is yours about which you want to be. Those of you who take this book seriously will prosper. Those of you who don't, will fail. No one else is going to do it for you, not even the government.

These programs are not welfare. No one is going to hand you a check for doing nothing, just because you happen to exist and you need the money. This is a chance to earn your place at the top. The government and Al Lowry will be guiding you along the way.

You Have To Take The Initiative, though. Isn't that what life is all about? Here in the United States, we have the greatest, most prosperous, and most upwardly mobile society the world has ever known. Anyone from anywhere can come here and be whatever he or she wants to be.

SOME PEOPLE MAKE IT, BUT MOST PEOPLE NEVER DO. They spend their entire lives thinking about what they could have been, instead of becoming all that they could be. Which group do you fit into? Are you a dreamer or a doer?

USE ALL THE TOOLS YOU'VE GOT. If you want to be a winner, then working hard is not enough. The world is full of honest, hard-working but unsuccessful people. If you don't know what you're doing, then a lot of your effort will probably be wasted. You will make other people rich, but the chances are, you'll never really get anywhere yourself.

That's where this book comes in. Once you're ready to do the work, once you're excited about the idea of being successful and you're ready to make changes in your life, this book will make it easier for you.

THE WISE MAN, THE STUBBORN MAN AND THE FOOL were all digging for gold. They were using their bare hands, because that's all they had to work with and all they knew. Then one day, a merchant came along selling shovels.

The Wise Man immediately traded some of his gold for one of the shovels and began to dig faster and more efficiently than before. Soon, he had gotten back all the gold he had paid for the shovel and more. He kept on digging until he was rich.

The Stubborn Man refused to buy a shovel. He didn't want to spend his hard-earned gold. Digging by hand had always been good enough before and he refused to change. He dug until his hands were raw and bleeding and then took his small pile of gold and went home to hoard it away. He died poor, but proud.

The Fool gave up all his gold to buy two shovels, since he thought two would dig twice as fast as one, and then immediately stopped digging. He wanted the shovels to dig for him, while he sat around and smoked his pipe. He sat there until he starved to death and then the Wise Man and the Stubborn Man used his own shovels to bury him.

I like to think of myself as that merchant and this book as the shovel you need if you are going to dig for gold. It won't do the work for you, but it certainly will make it a lot easier than digging by hand.

Which of the three men are you? The Wise Man, the Stubborn Man, or the Fool? The choice is yours. Now it's up to you to go for the gold.

KEY POINTS TO REMEMBER

1. Becoming successful is up to you.
2. Knowledge alone is not enough.
3. It takes effort and dedication to be a success.
4. The subconscious mind controls our lives and our destinies.
5. Wanting to change is not always enough.

AUTHOR'S NOTE

Most of the examples in this book are from my own experience and I know they work. Some of the examples have been reported to me by my friends and graduates—I have confidence that they are reliable.

Notwithstanding the above, the fifty states each have different laws and different regions have various interpretations of laws, rules, and regulations. I strongly advise you to research your own local situation before you enter into any contracts. If you are not absolutely sure of your ground in any real estate situation, seek the help of professional advisors.

If I can be of help to you with additional material or you wish to enroll in one of my seminars or other programs, please write to me at 3390 Duesenberg Drive, Westlake Village, CA 91362 or call 805-496-4400.

Albert Lowry

ABOUT THE AUTHOR

The author of several best-selling real estate books, Dr. Albert Lowry is founder and chief executive of the Education Advancement Institute, which holds real estate education seminars every week in hundreds of cities across the United States and Canada. Since 1971, more than 200,000 Americans have taken Lowry seminars. Raised in an orphanage, Dr. Lowry went on to become a self-made millionaire in real estate. He is the father of five children and works in Westlake Village, California.

INDEX

243